Dogs

Rex Marchant

Macdonald/Educational

Managing Editor Chris Milsome
Series Editor Verity Weston
Editor Anne Furniss
Design Peter Benoist
Production Philip Hughes

First published 1974
Reprinted 1978
Macdonald Educational
Holywell House
Worship Street
London EC2A 2EN

contents

ISBN 0 356 04457 2

© Macdonald Educational Limited 1974

Printed in Belgium by
Henri Proost, Turnhout,
Belgium.

Man and dog an ancient partnership

The first steps to friendship

According to an old legend, during the creation of the world the earth split. Adam was left on one side, with the animals on the other. The dog jumped over the gap to stand beside him, and so the two became friends.

No-one really knows how or when man and the dog became friends. Dogs' bones have been found in prehistoric camp sites dating from about 9000 B.C., but the relationship may be even older than that.

Guard and hunter

The first dogs to make friends with man were probably more like the wolves or jackals of today. Perhaps they crept near the camp sites of early man at night, looking for scraps of food. Gradually man would realize that this gave him some protection, warning him of more ferocious animals which lurked in the night.

Soon, a partnership may have been formed. Man and dog may have begun to hunt together. The swift-footed dogs could outrun the prey and drive it back to the man, who would kill it with primitive weapons.

These two services, of guard and hunting companion, made the dog very valuable to man and have remained its most important duties. Since those early times many animals have been tamed, but only the dog has earned the title of "man's best friend".

▶ Man's first friend was the dog. Cave paintings such as this one found in Algeria prove that the dog has been man's ally since very ancient times.

◀ Beware of the dog. The message of this old Roman mosaic from Pompeii is very clear. Guarding his home or campsite was one of the earliest tasks the dog performed for man, and remains one of the most usual.

CAVE CANEM

◀ "The Lifesaver Dog". This 1914 magazine picture is supposed to illustrate a real event. Many stories have been told of the courage and loyalty of the dog.

▼ The hunting dog has always been valued. When man began to hunt for pleasure rather than through necessity, he started to breed specialized dogs.

Down from the trees evolution

Bat-eared fox

Dhole

Bush dog

Cape hunting dog

▲ The bat-eared fox lives in desert areas of Southern Africa.

▲ The South American bush dog looks rather like a badger. It dives and swims well.

▲ The dhole lives in Asia and is untameable. It is small and hunts in packs.

▲ Cape Hunting dogs hunt in packs, relying on stamina rather than speed.

1 million years

10 million years

Cynodictis

35 million years

Miacis

50 million years

Millions of years of dogs

Both men and dogs have ancestors that lived in trees. *Miacis* was the ancestor of all carnivores (animals which eat meat, such as the dog). It had short, heavy legs and a very long tail.

Over millions of years, the descendants of *Miacis* slowly changed their habits and shape until a new animal evolved: *Cynodictis*. Changes continued to take place and eventually produced *Tomarctus*, the first animal to look like a true dog.

From *Tomarctus* sprang all the present day members of the dog family. However, there was a split in the chain quite early on, so some animals, such as the Cape hunting dog, are only very distant relatives of the true dogs.

A missing link

After *Tomarctus* there must have been an animal which was the immediate ancestor of the domestic dog, but its remains have not yet been found. Both the wolf and the dog may be descended from this missing link, but some scientists believe the dog is descended from a small wolf which has since become extinct. Another theory is that the dog may be a cross between a wolf and a jackal.

Although we know so much about its very distant past, the dog's recent history remains shrouded in mystery.

Fox

Wolf

Jackal

Wild dog

Domestic dog

▲ Despite much argument, most experts now agree that the fox is a true dog.

▲ There are various kinds of jackal. They hunt or scavenge for their food.

▲ Becoming domesticated has moved the dog a bit further away from its relatives.

▲ There are nine species of wolf living in many different parts of the world.

▲ In the forests of South America there are many little-known species of wild dog.

Tomarctus

▲ *Tomarctus* looked more like a modern dog, but was probably not as intelligent.

◀ Changes in *Miacis* produced *Cynodictis*. It spent more time on the ground and was better fitted for running.

◀ Dogs and cats are both descended from *Miacis,* a tree-climbing animal about the size of a mink.

How the dog evolves

▼ How animals develop depends very much on how and where they live. In forests, small features and short legs are an advantage. This bush dog can easily slip through the undergrowth.

▲ In deserts and plains, animals travel long distances at speed and become lean and long-legged. The bat-eared fox has developed large, pointed ears which pick up distant sounds.

This is a dog

All shapes and sizes

If we ever had visitors from outer space, it would be difficult for them to believe that the tiny Chihuahua and the huge St. Bernard belonged to the same species. No other animal shows such a variation in appearance as the dog. An adult toy dog might be only 127 mm. (5 in.) tall at the shoulder, but an Irish Wolfhound, also an adult, might be 0.9 m. (3 ft.) tall.

But all dogs are built to the same basic plan. Apart from the tail, their skeletons only vary in size and proportion. They have the same number of teeth and the same average temperatures. Their puppies grow up in the same way, even though the puppies of one breed might be larger than the adults of another breed!

The ages of dog and man

There used to be a theory that one year of a dog's life was equal to seven human years, but few people believe this now. It has been pointed out that at one year a dog is adult, but at seven years a human is not.

If you want to work out the age of a dog, most experts would suggest the following table:

6 dog months equal 10 human years
1 dog year equals 15 human years
2 dog years equal 24 human years

After that, each dog year equals four human years.

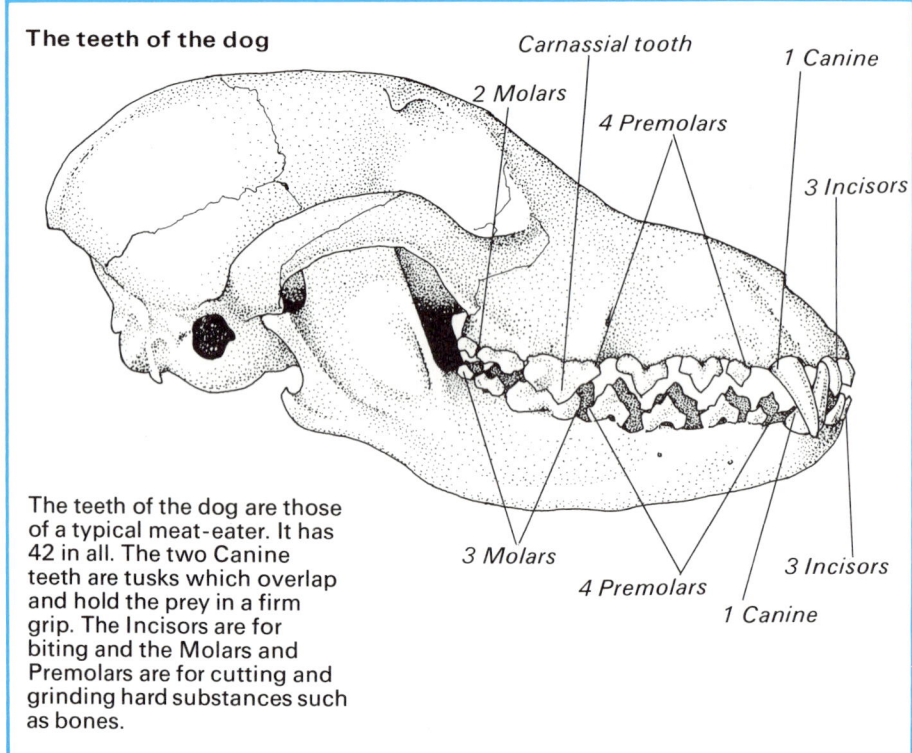

The teeth of the dog

The teeth of the dog are those of a typical meat-eater. It has 42 in all. The two Canine teeth are tusks which overlap and hold the prey in a firm grip. The Incisors are for biting and the Molars and Premolars are for cutting and grinding hard substances such as bones.

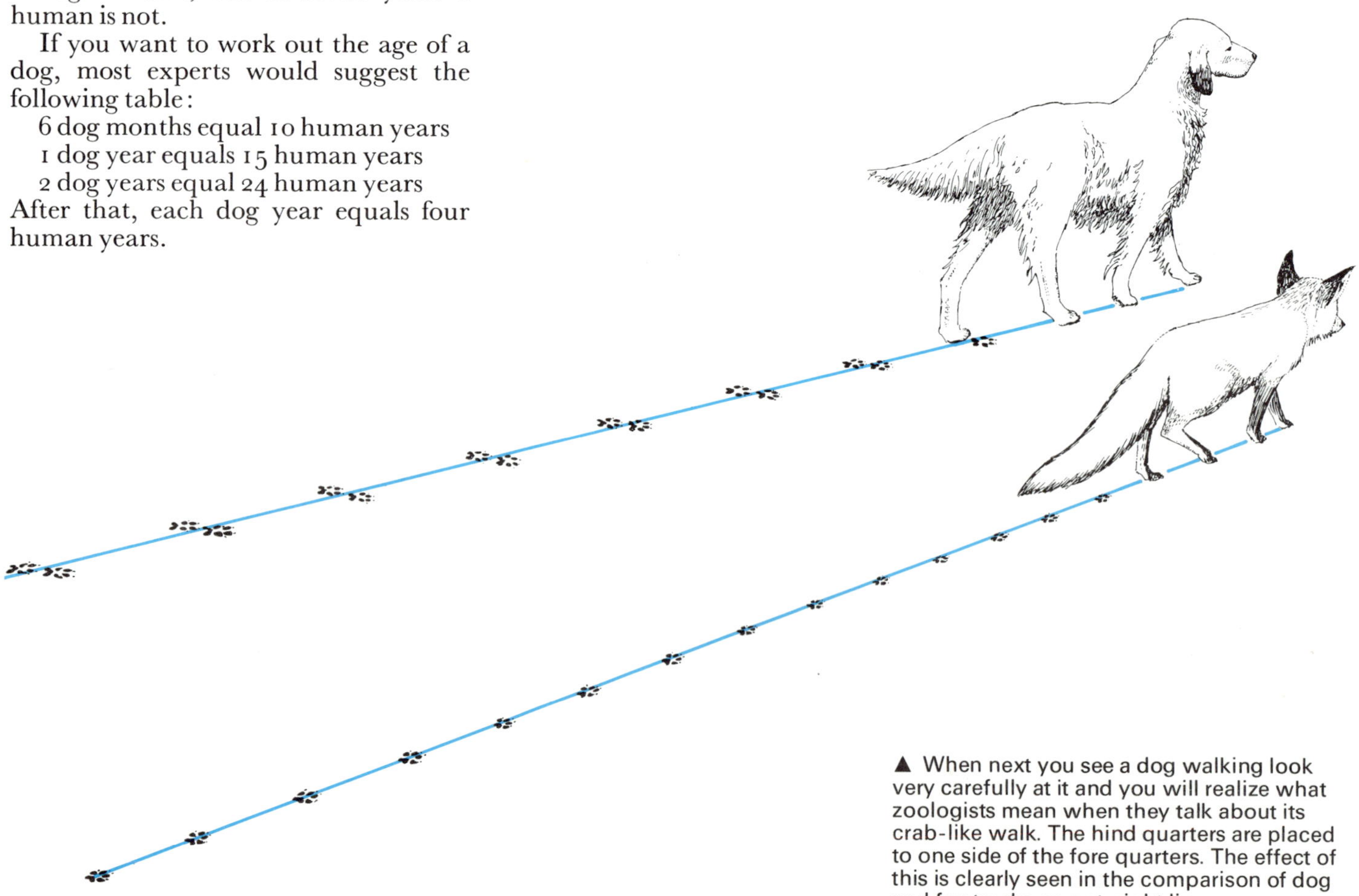

Carnassial tooth · 2 Molars · 4 Premolars · 1 Canine · 3 Incisors · 3 Molars · 4 Premolars · 1 Canine · 3 Incisors

▲ When next you see a dog walking look very carefully at it and you will realize what zoologists mean when they talk about its crab-like walk. The hind quarters are placed to one side of the fore quarters. The effect of this is clearly seen in the comparison of dog and fox tracks on a straight line.

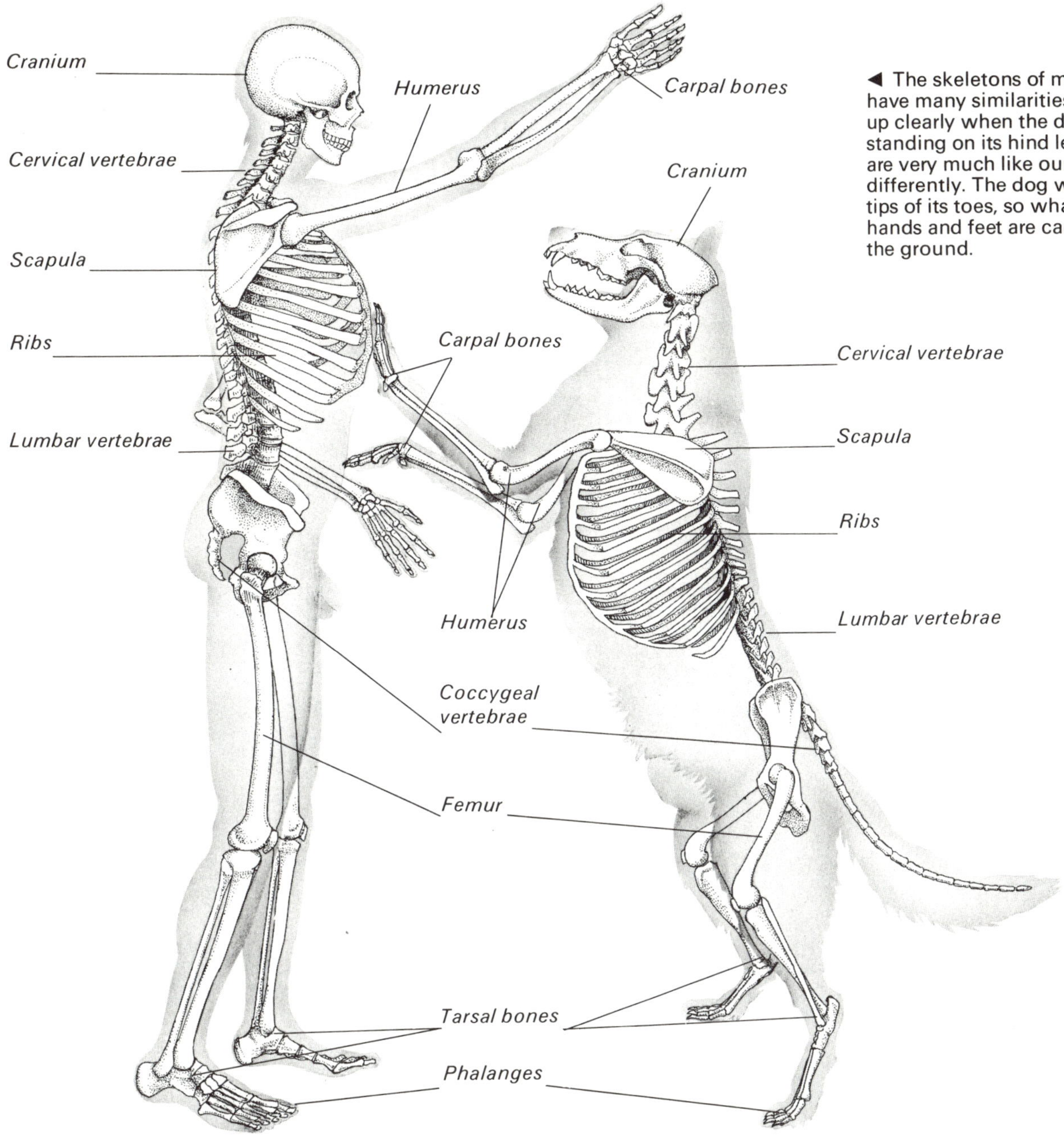

Cranium

Humerus

Carpal bones

Cervical vertebrae

Cranium

Scapula

Carpal bones

Cervical vertebrae

Ribs

Scapula

Lumbar vertebrae

Ribs

Humerus

Lumbar vertebrae

Coccygeal vertebrae

Femur

Tarsal bones

Phalanges

◄ The skeletons of man and dog have many similarities. This shows up clearly when the dog is drawn standing on its hind legs. The limbs are very much like ours but are used differently. The dog walks on the tips of its toes, so what would be hands and feet are carried clear of the ground.

Three stages in the life of a dog

▲ The typical unsteady pose of a young puppy. Life can be frightening for puppies. They do not open their eyes until 9–12 days after birth and sometimes only two-thirds of a litter survive the first three weeks.

▲ A dog is considered to be mature at different ages in different breeds. This fully-grown Labrador is two years old. It is at the peak of its physical strength and may take up to 64 km. (40 miles) exercise a day.

▲ As it grows older, a dog begins to fill out and its facial hair turns white. The length of life also varies from breed to breed. Some only live eight years, but one Labrador reached the age of 27 years 4 months.

The savage kin wild dogs

Near dogs and true dogs

The relatives of the dog all belong to the family *Canidae*. As the map shows, they are spread over a major part of the world.

Experts disagree about how the dogs are related, but it is generally agreed that the true dogs (Canids) are wolves, jackals, foxes, some South American wild dogs and the domestic dog. Cape hunting dogs, bush dogs, dholes and bat-eared foxes are only distant relatives.

Hunters and scavengers

As well as looking very different, the members of the dog family behave in very different ways. Some, like the wolves and Cape hunting dogs, live and hunt in closely-knit packs. Others, such as the fox, hunt by themselves. These differences apply even within one species of dog. For instance, some jackals hunt for their food, but some scavenge, that is hang around the kills of larger animals waiting for leftover scraps.

One of the strangest members of the dog family is the raccoon-like dog of Asia, which fishes and climbs trees in search of fruit.

Key to map

	Foxes
	Wolves
	Wild dogs
	Jackals
	Bush dog
	Dhole
	Bat-eared fox
	Cape hunting dog

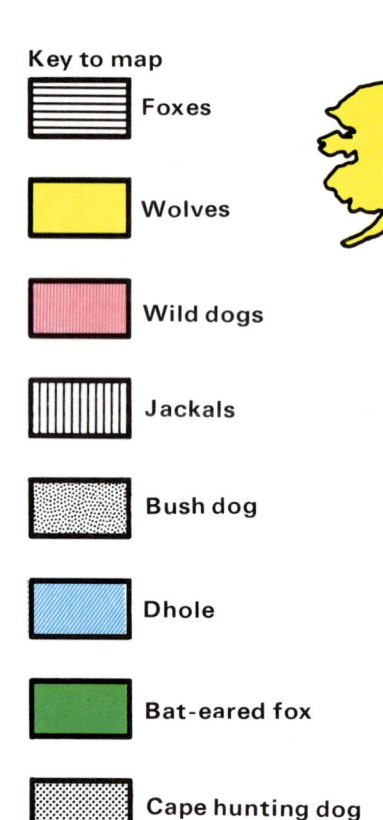

▲ Wolves dig out their own dens or enlarge ready-made hollows. They are good parents. Until the cubs are a few weeks old the male brings food to his mate. After that they look after the cubs together.

▼ A rare photograph of a pack of Cape hunting dogs on a hunt. Although renowned for their fierceness, these animals are surprisingly little known. This is because they have no fixed camps or dens but roam around in packs.

Map showing where wild dogs live

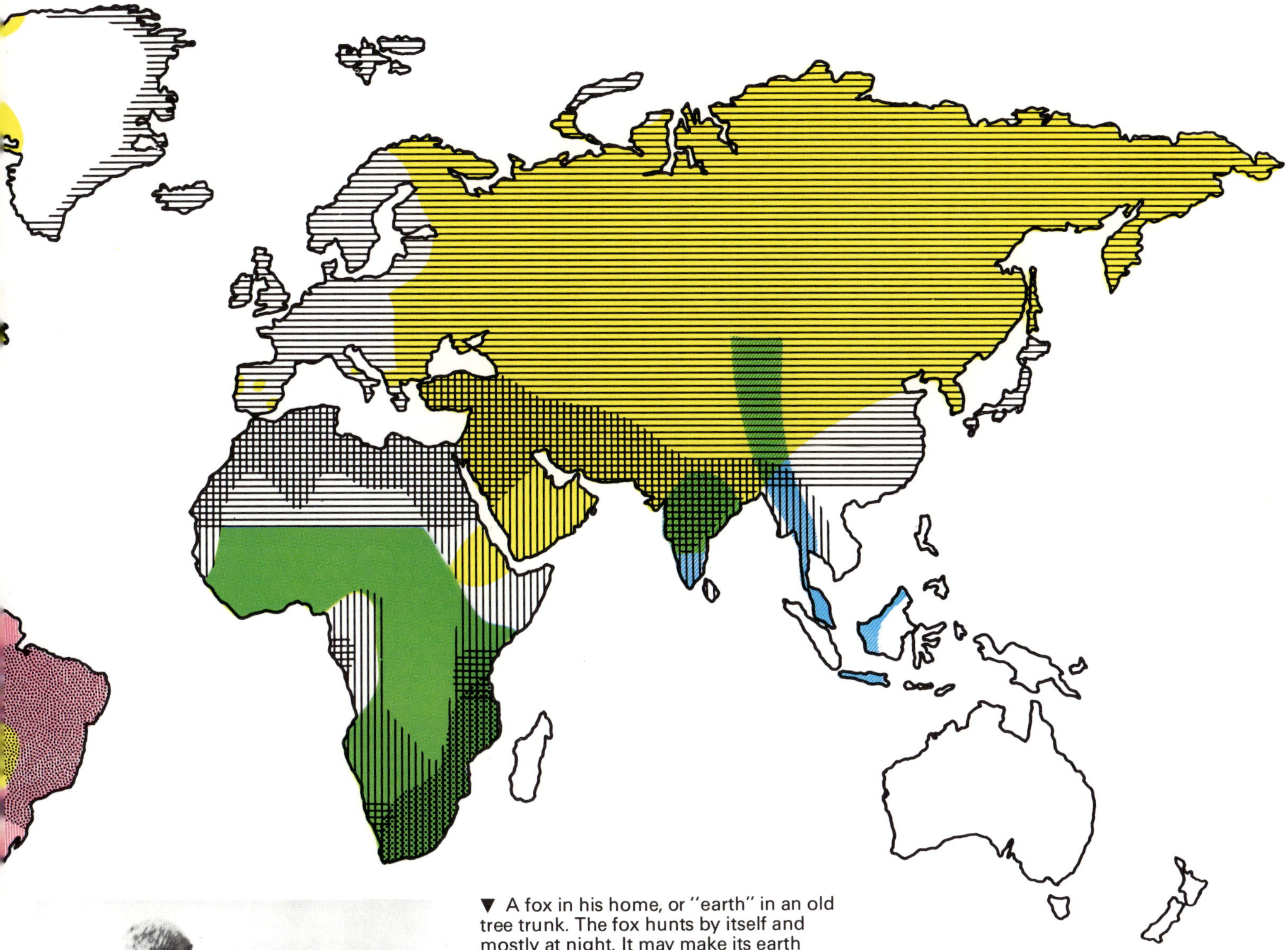

▼ A fox in his home, or "earth" in an old tree trunk. The fox hunts by itself and mostly at night. It may make its earth almost anywhere. Sometimes it takes over an old rabbit warren or a badger's set. It has even been known to live in trees.

▲ A jackal threatens a vulture which is approaching its food. The jackal normally scavenges for its food (that is eats the leftovers from the kills of other animals) but it can kill for itself if necessary.

Traces of the past

A different way of life

It is more than ten thousand years since the dog gave up its dangerous and uncertain life in the wilds and came to live with man. Since that day the dog has lived in a human community. In return for its services to man it has been fed and housed and no longer has to kill for itself. It now obeys the commands of a human master rather than those of a pack leader.

An unconscious heritage

In spite of this long history of life with man, the domestic dog still has many habits which are like those of its wild relatives. Many of these are quite useless in its domestic life, but the dog will still perform them. They are an unconscious reminder of an ancient way of life.

The drawings on this page show some of these strange characteristics.

► Dogs look on their master as their pack leader and will show him the same respect. They accept his family as members of the pack.

▲ Before dogs lie down to sleep they will often circle several times. Wild dogs do this to flatten the long grass in which they sleep.

▲ Dogs inherit a strong sense of territory and defend it fiercely. They are natural scavengers and will often investigate rubbish heaps.

▲ Wild dogs howl to keep in touch with their pack over long distances. When dogs howl in chorus it is often to ward off intruders.

▲ Dogs have a natural instinct to join up in packs.

▼ Dogs expecting a walk behave like wild dogs before a hunt. They work themselves up into a state of great excitement.

▼ One very common habit is to store extra food by burying it. In the wild, dogs cannot always rely on regular meals.

► Scent marking by leg lifting is common to all dogs as a way of marking territory. A domestic dog may do it 50—100 times on one walk.

▲ Wild dogs roll in dirt and dung to disguise their scents when hunting.

Survival means change

▲ A friendly grin seems to be something dogs have copied from humans. It is a greeting used only by domestic dogs, who use it just to greet human beings and never with other dogs.

A great ability to change

Dogs are among the most successful animals in the world. This means that, despite difficulties, they have been able to survive and increase their numbers.

The reason dogs are so successful is that they are able to alter their way of life to fit in with changing conditions. When their normal prey becomes scarce, hunting dogs can learn to scavenge. Scavengers, in their turn, can learn to hunt.

The coyote is a type of wolf which lives in the United States. It used to live and hunt in packs, but as man spread across the country this became dangerous. So the coyote changed its way of life and became a true lone wolf. In this way it was able to survive.

▲ Because of the growth of towns and cities, foxes have been forced to change their habits. Many now live in towns or slink into them at night.

The biggest single change for the dog came when it started to live with man. Cave life was hard, but it was much easier than the wild. This caused changes in the bodies of the dogs, and scientists can separate wild dogs from early domestic dogs when they find them on ancient sites. As time went on the adult domestic dogs kept some features found only in wild dog pups, such as short legs and muzzles, floppy ears and hanging tails.

From *Molossus* to Bull Terrier

Molossus

◄ *Molossus,* a huge Mastiff-like dog, was
bred by the Romans for fighting and hunting.
It was also used as a guard dog.

Bulldog

▲ The Bulldog is a descendant of *Molossus*
through the Mastiff. With its iron grip, this
dog was ideal for the cruel but popular sport
of bull baiting.

Making a new breed

For centuries, men have been breeding
dogs for special purposes. The adaptable nature of the dog has made this
easy. If a small, brave dog was needed
for a special type of hunting, a small dog
crossed with a dog with a reputation for
courage often produced the required
result.

An example of a man-made breed is
the modern Bull Terrier, whose history
is explained in pictures on this page.

Cross-breeding has produced many
popular and useful breeds of dog, but it
has also had some unfortunate side-effects. The loose skin and droopy ears
of the Basset Hound are a result of cross-breeding. This floppy skin gives the
dogs a comical appearance, but the long
ears make hearing difficult.

Because of this, there are now very
strict regulations about breeding.

Bull-and-Terrier

▲ When bull baiting was banned, its
followers turned to dog fighting. The
powerful Bulldog was crossed with the
quick-witted Terrier to produce the Bull-and-Terrier, a dog well-fitted for this sport.

White English Terrier

▲ In the mid-19th century, breeders crossed
the Bull-and-Terrier with the White English
Terrier, a breed which is now extinct. This
eventually produced the Bull Terrier.

Bull Terrier

Origins of the breeds

Where the family developed

The Dingo group

The Dingo lives in the wild, but it was probably one of the first dogs to befriend man. It is believed to have travelled to Australia with early man. Half the world's dogs belong to the Dingo group, but the only domestic breeds are the Basenji and the Rhodesian ridgeback.

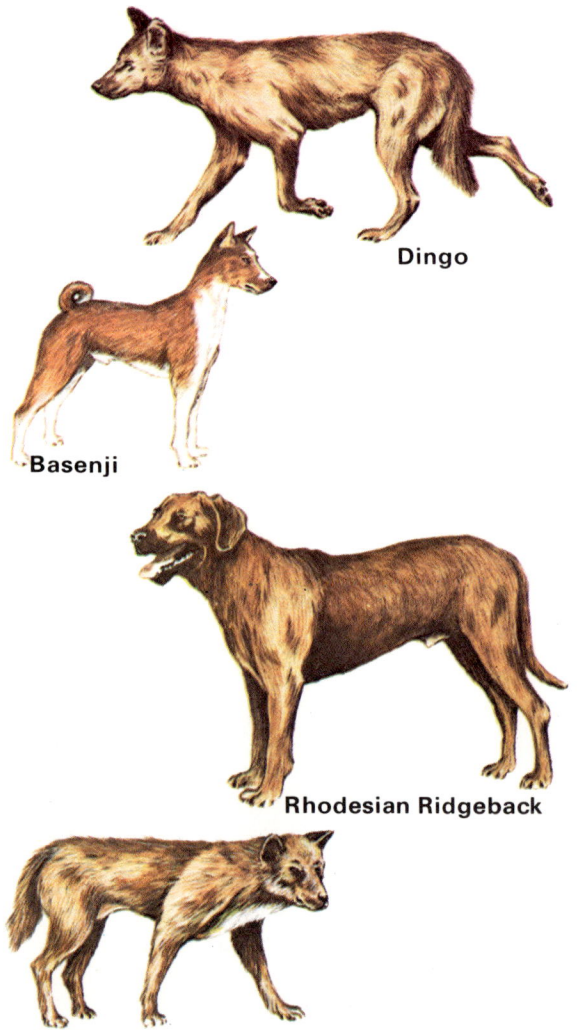

Dingo

Basenji

Rhodesian Ridgeback

New Guinea Singing Dog

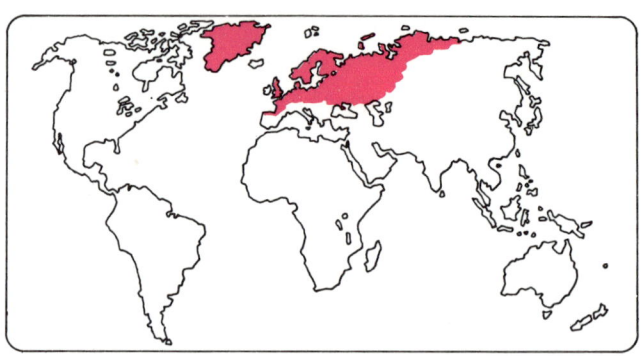

The Northern group

This group of dogs is thought to be descended from the large grey wolves of Northern Europe. Not only sledge dogs but the world's best sheepdogs belong to this group, including the Alsatian and the Collie. Terriers are also included in this group, although they are only distantly related.

Husky

Keeshond

Kerry Blue

Old English Sheepdog

The Greyhound group

These dogs are especially suited to hunting in open country. The group originated in the deserts of North Africa and Asia. The basic Greyhound shape has survived in all members of the family and the breeds only vary in coat and size. There was probably a single ancestor of much the same build.

Afghan

Ibizan hound

Scottish Deerhound

Italian Greyhound

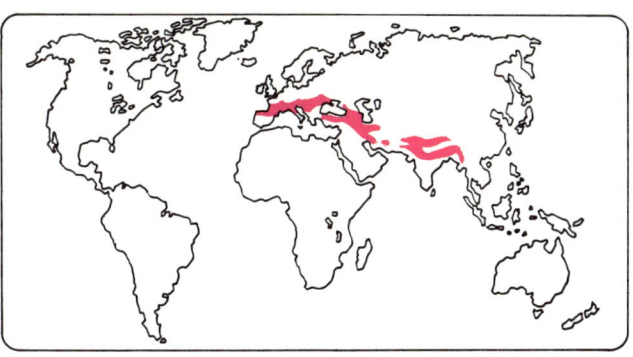

The Mastiff group

The many differences between these breeds show that they are descended from several types of animal. The group originally came from the mountains running across Europe and Asia. Although their looks vary so much, these dogs are all noted for their powers of scent.

Great Dane

Japanese Spaniel

Basset Hound

Dalmatian

It's a dog's life

World-wide dog mania

To be treated like a dog or to live a dog's life are phrases which suggest a miserable existence. But there are millions of people who do not get as much food and care as some pet dogs.

Many people will themselves go without so that their dogs can still live well. In primitive countries facing food shortages, stories have been reported of dogs being fed while old people are left to starve.

In richer parts of the world, dogs are sometimes treated as if they were people. They have their own hotels, hospitals and cemeteries. In Germany, a dog can even be covered by insurance so that it will be looked after if its owner dies.

On the other hand, there are many cases of cruelty and thousands of unwanted dogs are abandoned each year.

Working for a living

While strays scavenge and pets often live in the lap of luxury, many dogs work hard for a living. Until quite recently, many tradesmen in Europe had dog-drawn carts to deliver their goods. In parts of Canada, mail used to be delivered in dog sledges.

Many other jobs have been found for dogs. They race, fight, hunt and even get eaten, all for man's pleasure. A dog's life can mean many things.

▲ "Love me, love my dog": an old saying which could well apply to this picture from Bangladesh. All over the world, the dog is accepted as one of the family.

◄ But no-one seems to want this little puppy. Many dogs are bought as Christmas presents and then turned out when they become unwanted.

▲ A one-woman rescue service. This elderly Englishwoman, known as Camberley Kate, devotes her life to caring for stray dogs.

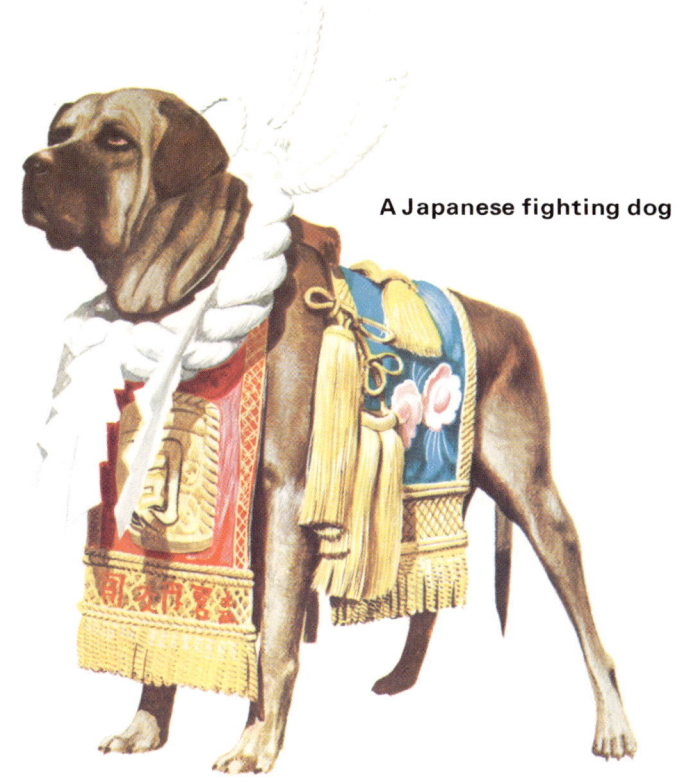

A Japanese fighting dog

▲ A 19th century dog thief. Pet dogs were often stolen and then a ransom was demanded from their owners.

▲ A Japanese fighting dog in champion's costume. Although banned in some countries, dog fighting is very popular in others.

▲ Not everyone is a dog lover. As this 1813 print shows, dogs were used as crocodile bait in Egypt.

◄ Dog on sale in a butcher's shop. This picture was taken in China in 1966. In countries where food is scarce, the dog is regarded as a source of meat rather than as a pet.

The hunting dog

The dog has a smaller field of vision than the rabbit. This gives the prey a chance and so keeps nature's balance.

Area of vision

Gaze-hounds and scent hounds

Dogs are natural hunters and man must have used them as such long before he found any other purpose for them. Very little would have been expected of these early hunting dogs. They would have used the same tactics as they did in the wild.

Hunting dogs still fit into the two main groups that have existed for thousands of years. One group is made up of gaze-hounds; the other of scent hounds. Having sighted game, members of the first group rely on speed to run it down. Gaze-hounds came originally from the deserts of the Middle East, and the Greyhound is a typical example.

For the scent hound the nose is much more important than the eyes. Gun dogs and the various hounds that hunt in packs are all scent hounds. These developed in Europe, where the mild climate and thick undergrowth made scenting easier than sighting.

Made to measure

Since prehistoric times, man has bred many different types of hunting dog, each tailor-made for a particular job.

With its short legs, the Basset Hound can move through dense cover to flush out game; but it cannot run too fast and so outstrip hunters following on foot. Terriers are so called from the Latin word *terra*, meaning earth. They were sent into a burrow after a fox or badger when it went to ground.

Dogs have been bred to hunt beasts ranging from lions to hares and to be at home on every type of ground.

▲ Running down the desert gazelles is the sport for which the Saluki has been bred. Some say that this dog is the same type as the first swift dogs used by man.

▶ This old print shows stag hunting with pairs of Greyhounds. This sport has gradually died out, and Greyhounds are better known today as racing dogs.

▲ The Spaniel is an ancient hunting breed used both to flush game and to retrieve it. Duck or geese are brought back from water or marsh.

▼ Pointers are so called because when they find game they freeze and stand with head pointing towards it, with one leg bent.

◄ Raccoon hunting is an American sport which takes place at night. Coonhounds chase raccoons up trees and hold them for the hunters.

▲ A Dachshund digs after a badger. In its homeland of Germany the Dachshund has always been regarded as a hunting dog and has even been used against wild boar.

◄ A French pack of Beagles getting ready to set off. The Beagle is a hound that hunts by scent and in a pack. Hares are the usual quarry.

A world of smells the senses

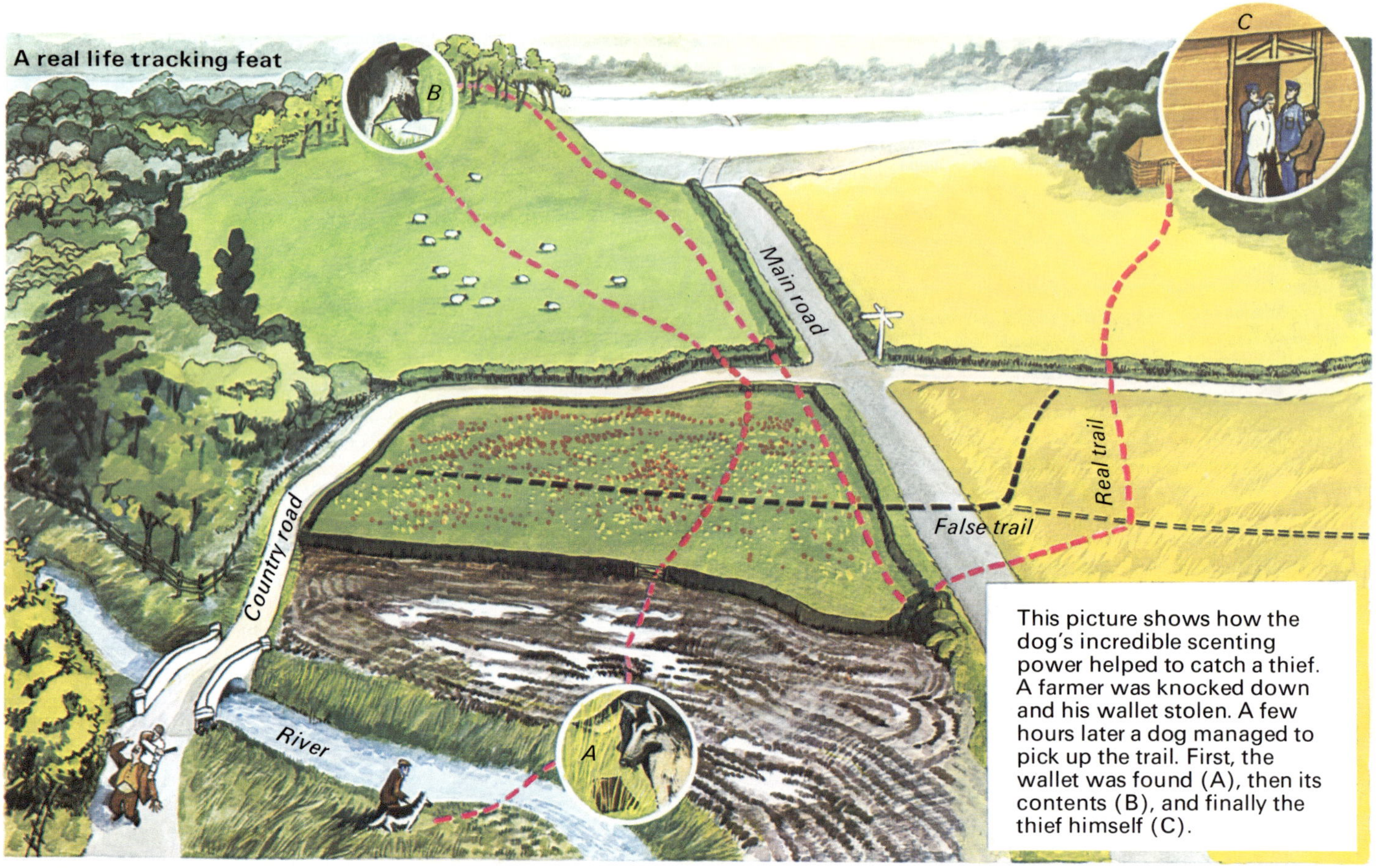

A real life tracking feat

This picture shows how the dog's incredible scenting power helped to catch a thief. A farmer was knocked down and his wallet stolen. A few hours later a dog managed to pick up the trail. First, the wallet was found (A), then its contents (B), and finally the thief himself (C).

Country road

Main road

River

False trail

Real trail

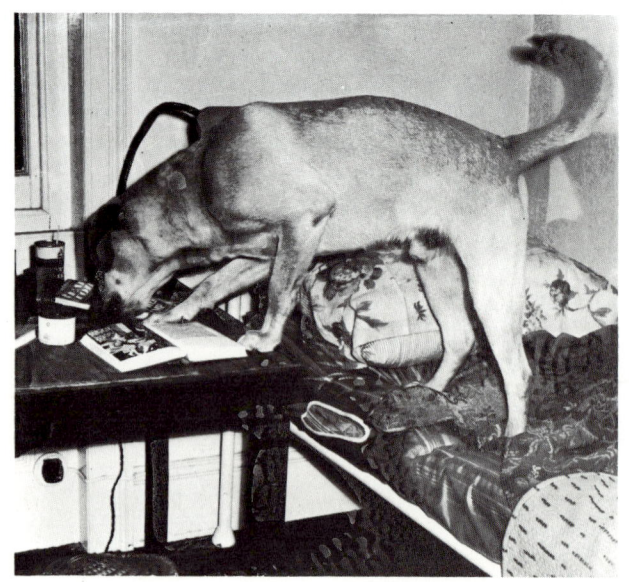

▲ It does not matter how carefully packets of drugs may have been hidden, this specially trained dog will sniff them out. In recent years customs and police forces have used many dogs in this work.

▲ These dogs are truffle hunters. Truffles, which are used to flavour cooking, grow underground and are therefore difficult to find. Dogs are sometimes used to sniff them out.

Led by the nose

To the wild animal, which either hunts or is hunted, the senses are all-important. Most animals have one sense which is more developed than the others, and with the dog it is the sense of smell.

This incredible sense varies from breed to breed, but in all cases it is much better than that of man. Where a man has about five million cells used for smelling, an Alsatian has over 200 million.

Tests have also proved that the dog uses its nose more efficiently than man. A healthy dog can detect a single drop of blood in 5.6 litres (10 pints) of water.

Despite the amazing power of its nose, local conditions can still make it difficult for a dog to follow tracks. Hot sun, strong wind, rain, frost or snow all help the prey to get away as they spoil the scent.

A flat, black-and-white world

Since a dog "sees" through its nose, it does not rely much on its not very good sight. Even dogs that hunt by sight have difficulty in seeing an animal if it stays still.

Scientists think that dogs see flat pictures rather than solid objects. They also think that dogs do not see colours, but various tones of black and white.

The dog's hearing is better developed than its sight, and is also better than man's hearing. Sounds that a man only four metres away does not hear are picked up by a dog at 25 metres. Their mobile ears make dogs much better than man at pin-pointing where a sound is coming from. They can also hear high-pitched sounds, which is why they respond to "silent" dog whistles.

Different ear shapes affect hearing

Irish Water Spaniel

Boston Terrier

◄ The hearing of dogs varies from breed to breed. Dogs with erect ears, like the Boston Terrier, can move them towards a sound, and have very acute hearing. But dogs with long-haired, drooping ears can have difficulty in hearing.

▼ Do dogs have a sixth sense? In 1902, the volcano above St. Pierre in Martinique erupted and destroyed the town. It is said that before the eruption the dogs in the town were very disturbed. This is one of many stories which suggest that dogs can pick up changes in the atmosphere.

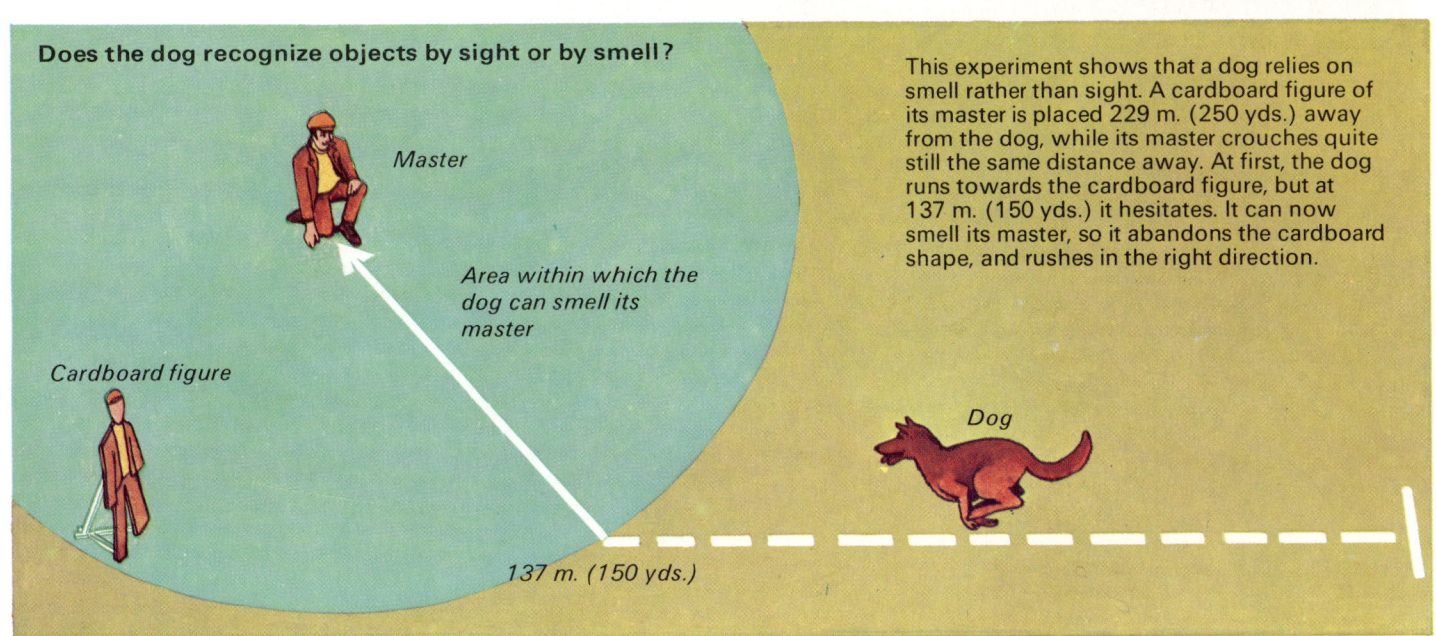

Does the dog recognize objects by sight or by smell?

Master

Area within which the dog can smell its master

Cardboard figure

Dog

137 m. (150 yds.)

This experiment shows that a dog relies on smell rather than sight. A cardboard figure of its master is placed 229 m. (250 yds.) away from the dog, while its master crouches quite still the same distance away. At first, the dog runs towards the cardboard figure, but at 137 m. (150 yds.) it hesitates. It can now smell its master, so it abandons the cardboard shape, and rushes in the right direction.

Dog meets dog communication

▲ Not just a funny face. The camera has frozen this man's expression in mid-sentence. It is from the millions of expressions which flit across our faces that the dog understands what we mean, not from the words we say.

A soundless language

It is natural that when we hear dogs bark we should imagine they are talking to one another. In fact, although barking is a form of communication it is not the main one. Most of what the dog wishes to say is said in an elaborate system of signs and body movements.

This method of exchanging information has some advantages. For one thing, users of such a non-verbal language cannot lie. A dog can tell from movements of the body, tail, ears, lips and eyes exactly what another dog is feeling at a given moment.

The dog which slinks, with ears back and tail between its legs, is being submissive. This means that it recognizes the dog to which it is making the movements as a superior animal. A stiff-legged approach with the tail held stiffly erect or wagging slowly is a challenge.

Scents and markings

The dog's system of body signals is helped out by a tremendous amount of information gained from scent. Many people think that it is only sexual interest that makes dogs sniff at each other. But body odours give away more than just sexual information.

Because of this, scent marking trees and posts with urine is very important. One smell at the base of a tree can tell a dog many things. It will know what sort of animals have left scents and even whether they were hungry or fully fed.

Man may have made the dog's methods of communication with its fellow dogs more difficult. An important part in the body language is played by markings on the dog's head and body. In his efforts to create new breeds, man may have bred out some of these different coloured patches and so destroyed part of the dog's "vocabulary".

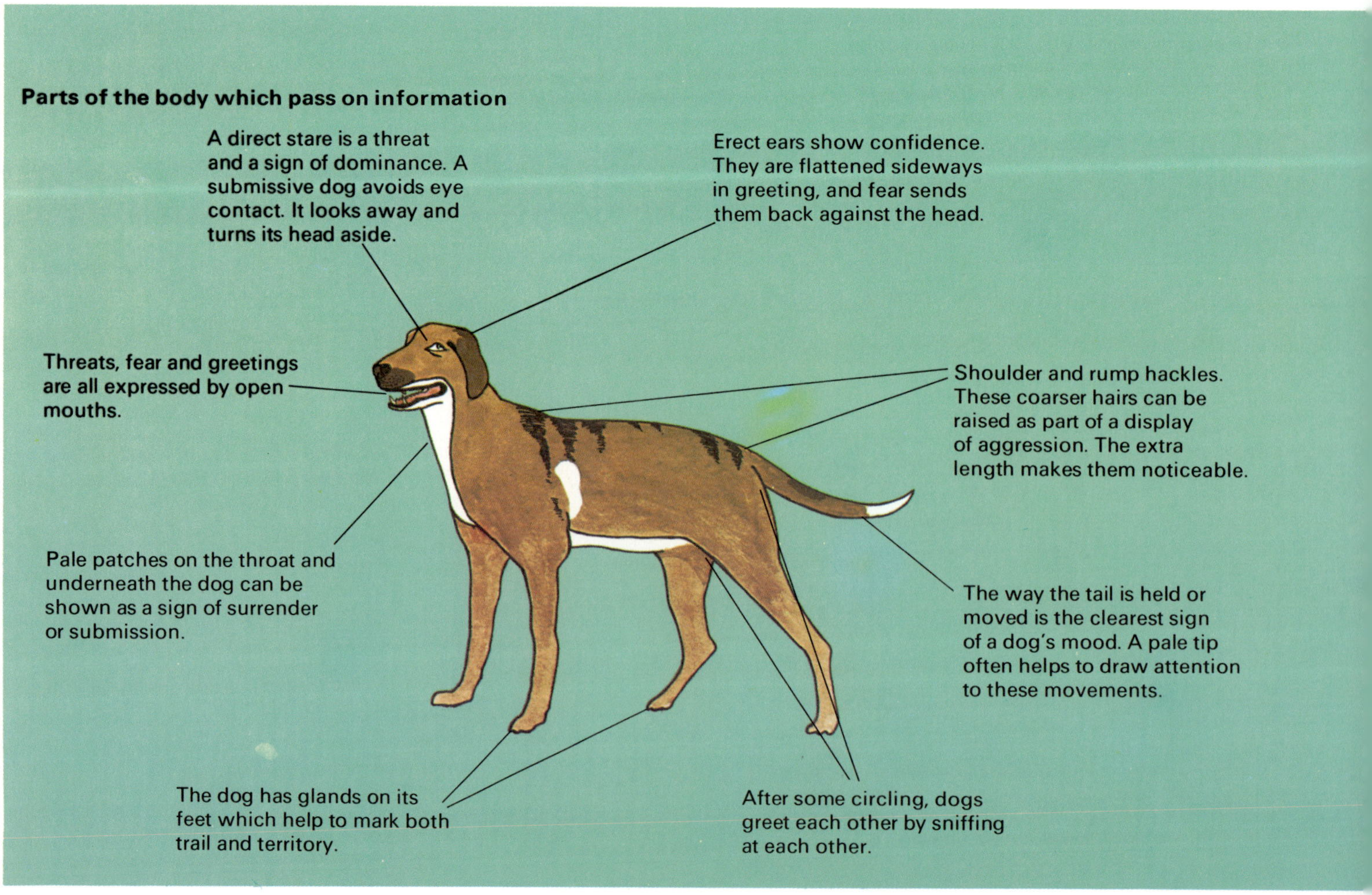

Parts of the body which pass on information

A direct stare is a threat and a sign of dominance. A submissive dog avoids eye contact. It looks away and turns its head aside.

Erect ears show confidence. They are flattened sideways in greeting, and fear sends them back against the head.

Threats, fear and greetings are all expressed by open mouths.

Shoulder and rump hackles. These coarser hairs can be raised as part of a display of aggression. The extra length makes them noticeable.

Pale patches on the throat and underneath the dog can be shown as a sign of surrender or submission.

The way the tail is held or moved is the clearest sign of a dog's mood. A pale tip often helps to draw attention to these movements.

The dog has glands on its feet which help to mark both trail and territory.

After some circling, dogs greet each other by sniffing at each other.

To the man this is just a tree, but to the dog it is more like a reference library. Scent traces show him how many animals have passed by and how long ago, what age and sex they were and whether they were injured or ill.

Facial expressions

▲ Facial expressions are an important means of communication. This shows the dog's normal, alert face.

▲ This dog is showing submission by pulling its lips back into a "submissive grin".

▲ The dog is frightened and angry. Ears back, it rolls up its lips to show its teeth in a "threat gape".

Dog meets dog

▲ These pictures show how two Cape hunting dogs behave on meeting each other. From the start, one dog takes up a dominant, or challenging, attitude, and approaches stiffly.

▲ The other dog realizes it has met a superior and shows its neck as a mark of submission, or respect. As the dominant dog gets closer, it lies down on its side.

23

Scientific guinea pigs

Testers and tasters

Dogs have been used in research ever since man began to be curious about the world he lived in. One of their first uses in this field was in the Middle Ages. They were made to test food in case it was poisoned.

Russian scientists are especially keen on using dogs in their research. This is because dogs have body systems very like those of man, and they stand up well to long experiments. Dogs were used in all the early space tests, and were the first living beings to be sent into outer space.

Pioneers or victims?

When doctors were forbidden to dissect human bodies, they used to cut up the bodies of dogs to find out about the workings of the body. It is in medical research that the dog has proved most useful to scientists. They have had almost every imaginable idea and substance tested on them.

In the past, there were no controls on live experiments and much suffering was caused. Many people have tried to have them banned. But live research has produced the cures for many diseases, so it may be a necessary evil.

First into space

Sputnik II

Laika in the space capsule

Mad dog!

▲ This old Persian print shows a man being bitten by a mad dog. In the past, the cry "mad dog" was enough to cause panic. These dogs had rabies, and a bite from a rabid dog could give people a fearful disease called hydrophobia, for which there was no cure.

► The first anti-rabies inoculation in 1885. On the left is Louis Pasteur, the brilliant French scientist who discovered a cure for the disease after years of research on dogs and other animals.

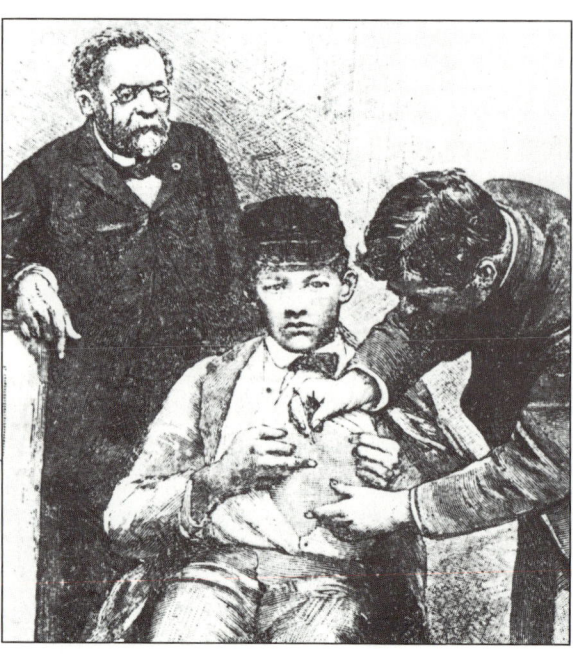

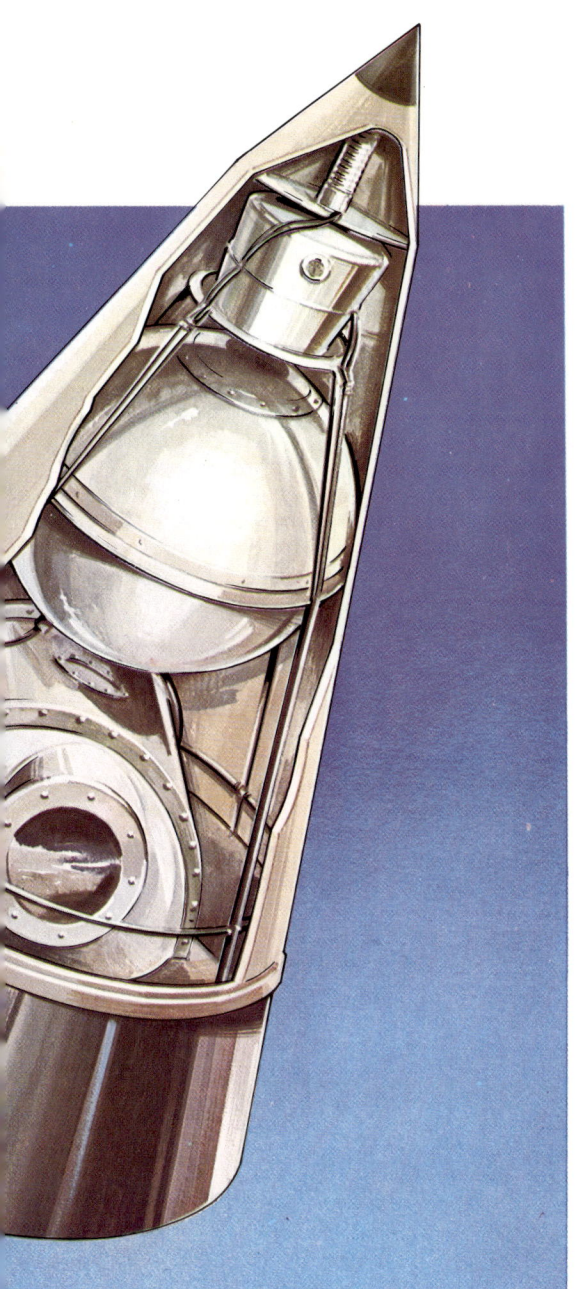

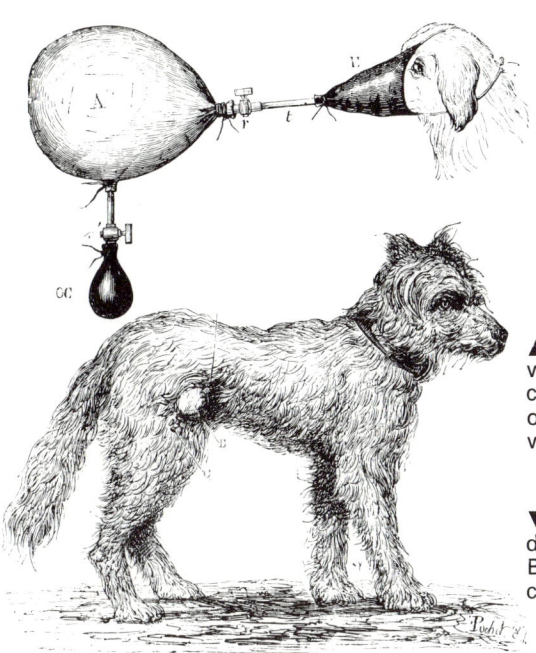

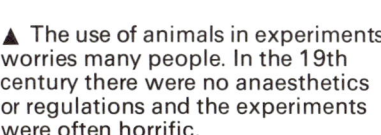

▲ The use of animals in experiments worries many people. In the 19th century there were no anaesthetics or regulations and the experiments were often horrific.

▼ Dr Banting (right) and the first dog to be cured of diabetes. Banting's work with dogs led to the control of the disease with insulin.

▲ The Russian Sputnik II was the first spacecraft to carry a living passenger into orbit about the earth. The historic date was November 3, 1957. The pioneer passenger was a small dog named Laika.

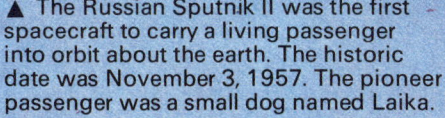

◄ This model on view in Moscow shows Laika in her capsule in the Sputnik. A mass of equipment sent full details of her flight to scientists in Russia.

Unfortunately, it was not possible to bring the spacecraft back to earth, so Laika died after her food supply ran out. Many people were upset by this, but the information obtained from the flight enabled scientists to send up more dogs and bring them safely back to earth.

It was due to these early experiments with animals that human beings were able to travel in space and survive.

D . . . O . . . G spells money

Big spenders

Dogs have become very big business in the modern world. A staggering amount of money is spent on them. According to one bank, in 1966 over three billion dollars was spent on pet dogs in the U.S. alone. The world total is beyond estimate.

The main items in the U.S. total were vets' fees and materials, food and the purchase of dogs. People who have paid a lot of money for a dog are prepared to spend more to keep it healthy.

But some people take this to extremes. As much as 450 million dollars was spent on clothes and accessories. Amongst the articles available for dog-wear are cosmetics, sunglasses, swim-suits and even roller skates. One man spent 1,700 dollars on a kennel with a gold drinking fountain for his Alsatian.

Dogs also affect the spending of vast sums of money in the worlds of sport and entertainment, and dog appeal is used to sell a vast number of goods. In New York there is even a restaurant specially for dogs. All over the world, people are earning their livings with the help of dogs.

▲ Performing dogs always attract crowds at circuses and shows. One of the most difficult stunts to teach a dog is to approach fire.

▼ This Great Dane is a champion and earns his keep with high stud fees. He is shown here with the amount of food he eats in one day.

▲ The original Rin-Tin-Tin, in a scene from *Jaws of Steel*, made in 1927. Very few animal film stars have achieved the fame of Rin-Tin-Tin, a character who has since been played by many dogs.

◄ Dog racing is popular in many parts of the world. Thousands of pounds change hands in bets on the results and winning dogs earn big money for their owners.

▲ This little Yorkshire Terrier seems quite unbothered by the paper curlers. Owners will go to great lengths in order to win prizes at a show.

▼ Cosmetics for dogs seems to be a growing business. Mistress and pet can have their hair tinted to the same shade, and some dogs are even fitted with false eyelashes.

▲ English Setters being judged at a major dog show. Winning a title at a big show adds greatly to the value of a dog and its offspring.

The pet food business

▲ This dog is enjoying his meal. He should do, because many big firms have spent vast sums in competing for his custom. Now that few dogs are fed on scraps the canned food market is worth fighting for. In Britain, six times as much is spent on pet foods as on baby foods.

Shaggy dog heroes of fiction

▲ The monstrous dogs with huge eyes that were mastered by the soldier in *The Tinder Box,* a story by Hans Christian Andersen. Each dog guarded a chest full of treasure and could only be removed by magic.

"Next thing you know, he'll want dinner music."

R. © 1972 NAT'L. News. Syn. 12-6   BAD ANDERSON

▲ Dougal, a character from the popular television show *The Magic Roundabout.*

▼ Snoopy, one of the heroes of the cartoon strip *Peanuts,* is world famous.

▲ This is Marmaduke, the canine hero of an American cartoon.

PEANUTS   2-3

SIGH

SCHULZ

Some remarkable dogs

The highlight of the variety show was a talking dog act between a Terrier and a Pekingese. The audience applauded madly. "What wonderful dogs", they all said. The owner of the dogs was rather embarrassed by all the praise and finally admitted that the act was a fake. "It is not such a good act as you think", he explained. "You see, the Pekingese is a ventriloquist."

The same Pekingese also very much enjoyed a game of cards. Someone seeing it in action for the first time was amazed. "How clever to be able to play cards like that", he said. But the owner of the dog did not agree. "He is not really a very good card player", he replied. "He always wags his tail when he picks up good cards."

These are two examples of the "shaggy dog" story, a joke form which is really a tall story with a twist at the end.

Dogs have always been a popular choice for the characters of stories, cartoons and films. These are often visually told shaggy dog stories, and the dogs in them show up all that is comic in our own lives. Walt Disney, in particular, has created many endearing dog characters in his cartoon films.

▲ A still from the Walt Disney film *The Lady and the Tramp,* about the loves of a pedigree Spaniel and a mongrel.

▼ *A Hundred and One Dalmatians.* The popularity of this Disney film raised the price of Dalmatians by as much as 300% for a while.

Pluto

▲ The first and most famous of Walt Disney's cartoon dogs was Pluto. He was mischievous and stupid but filled with a good humour which no troubles could alter.

The dog as god ... or devil

◄ Chinese Fo dogs, kept by many people to bring luck and scare off evil spirits. These good luck charms were made in the form of the lion dog, a Chinese breed. Fo is the Chinese for Buddha, whose symbol is the lion.

A Chinese Fo dog

The worship of dogs

People in ancient times worshipped gods in many forms. Often these were in the image of animals which seemed powerful or frightened them, such as wolves and jackals. These gods had special priests who wore animal masks, and sacred animals would be kept in their temples. So many sacred dogs were kept in some temples that they seemed more like huge kennels than places of worship.

Dogs have played a part in tribal religions in various parts of the world. The Kalangs of Borneo kept red dogs in their homes and had wooden images of these dogs which they used in religious ceremonies.

In Nepal there used to be a festival at which a dog was worshipped. This was a happy occasion and garlands of flowers were hung about the necks of all the dogs in the country.

Anubis

▲ Anubis, the guardian of the dead, was one of the many animal gods of ancient Egypt. He is shown either as a dog or a jackal-headed man. This image guarded the tomb of the boy king, Tutankhamen.

► This wooden statue, called Wow-wow, sits on the edge of an Indian village in Canada. There is no better guard than a dog, so a dog image was chosen to protect the village from evil spirits.

Wow-wow

Hellhounds and dogheads

In the past, dogs have also been the subject of some terrifying stories and superstitions. Because of the heathen worship of dogs, early Christians associated dogs with the devil. They thought the devil appeared to people in the shape of a black dog with curly hair, fiery eyes and long, pointed fangs.

Equally fearful were the stories of dogheaded giants, which were supposed to live in the East. They were thought to have dog heads on human bodies. Many of these stories were told to frighten people and, of course, no part-dog, part-human giants ever existed.

▲ The devil appears in the shape of a terrifying dog with flashing eyes. This scene take place in a mediaeval legend called *Faust*.

Cerberus

A werewolf

▲ According to legend, the entrance to Hades, the Greek underworld, was guarded by Cerberus, a terrible three-headed dog. The dead had to throw him a gift before he would let them pass.

◀ In the past, many people firmly believed in werewolves. These were supposed to be people who changed into dogs or wolves at night and went about hunting for victims.

In the service of man

▲ In this old print the dog's job is to run in its cage. This pulls ropes which turn the spit and cook the meat over the fire.

A creature of many talents

The partnership of man and dog has lasted centuries. Apart from the great friendship which has grown up between them, the main reason for this is the usefulness of the dog.

Dogs work for man in many different ways and, because the jobs vary, the dogs should not be compared. A dog guarding sheep in cold mountain pastures needs strength and stamina, whereas a dog which drives sheep from place to place needs speed and quick wits. Both do their own jobs very well, but neither would be capable of doing the other job.

Dog on the side of law and order

One of the finest examples of the working dog is the police dog, whose job includes many different tasks. An exciting chase after a fleeing criminal is rare, but a tracker dog will often lead police to a suspect. It will find important clues which may lead to the capture of a criminal. Many missing people are also found by the dogs each year.

High standards

Only 4 out of 100 dogs pass the tests to become a police dog. Vital qualities for the job are good health, intelligence, strength and a steady character. The breed which seems to combine the best of these is the Alsatian. When properly trained, these intelligent dogs are fearless, reliable and faithful to one master.

When a dog has been chosen, it goes immediately to live with its handler. This is the start of a partnership which will last its entire career. Each dog trains, works and lives with its handler. When it becomes too old to work, it will probably end its days as his pet.

▲ More than 2,000 travellers in the Alps have been saved by the famous St. Bernard dogs. The dogs were bred for this purpose by monks of the St. Bernard Hospice. Most rescues are now carried out with helicopters.

◀ Rusty is a detective specializing in plane crashes. He has been trained to find and retrieve clues, including flight recorders, which may help to pin-point the causes of air disasters.

Training a police dog

Police dogs were first used in Belgium in 1899 when the police chief of the city of Ghent had too few men to patrol at night. His answer was to use dogs and they were so successful that the idea spread. Now most police forces use dogs. Their training only varies slightly from place to place.

▲ Police dogs are taught to attack and hold suspects who try to resist, but to let go and stand off when they give in. The dogs are never out of control.

▼ Clearing the 2 m. (6 ft.) fence is a regular part of the police dog's training. When it can no longer manage it, the dog is retired.

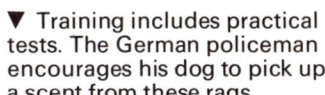

▲ Tracking is a most important job. A long rope checks the dog in training. On duty it can follow the scent freely.

▼ Training includes practical tests. The German policeman encourages his dog to pick up a scent from these rags.

From darkness into light guide dogs

New eyes and a new life

A job which has earned more respect and admiration for the dog than any other is that of guide dog to blind people. The praise heaped upon these dogs is well deserved, for they give new eyes and an active life to many handicapped people.

Only a dog, of all the animals domesticated by man, has the right qualities for this work. It is the final test of the friendship between dog and human being.

There are many old stories of blind beggars who kept pet dogs to help them, but it was not until this century that the idea developed into a well-planned scheme. The first school to train guide dogs was founded in Germany in 1916, and since then the idea has spread to many other parts of the world.

Trained from birth

A guide dog's work is very different from that of a police dog, but some of the same qualities are needed, so the Alsatian is good at this job. Another breed which is equally successful is the Labrador Retriever, as it is eager to please, placid and intelligent.

Training begins early, and selected puppies are reared in a family atmosphere where they are given simple obedience training. At ten months they are sent to a training centre.

The most important moment comes when the dog meets its future handler. This person has also spent some time training for a new way of life. Gradually a friendship builds up and they begin to understand one another. Finally, dog and handler leave the centre and enter the outside world together.

▶ Road drill is vital. The dog sits at the edge of the pavement until the command "Forward" is given. It then crosses the road at right angles. But the dog must also be taught to take no notice of this command if approaching traffic makes it unsafe to cross.

A walk with a guide dog

◀ A trainer teaches a dog to go round obstacles which are too low or narrow for the handler to pass. When the handler is with him and the path is blocked, the dog will sit to show that it is going into the road.

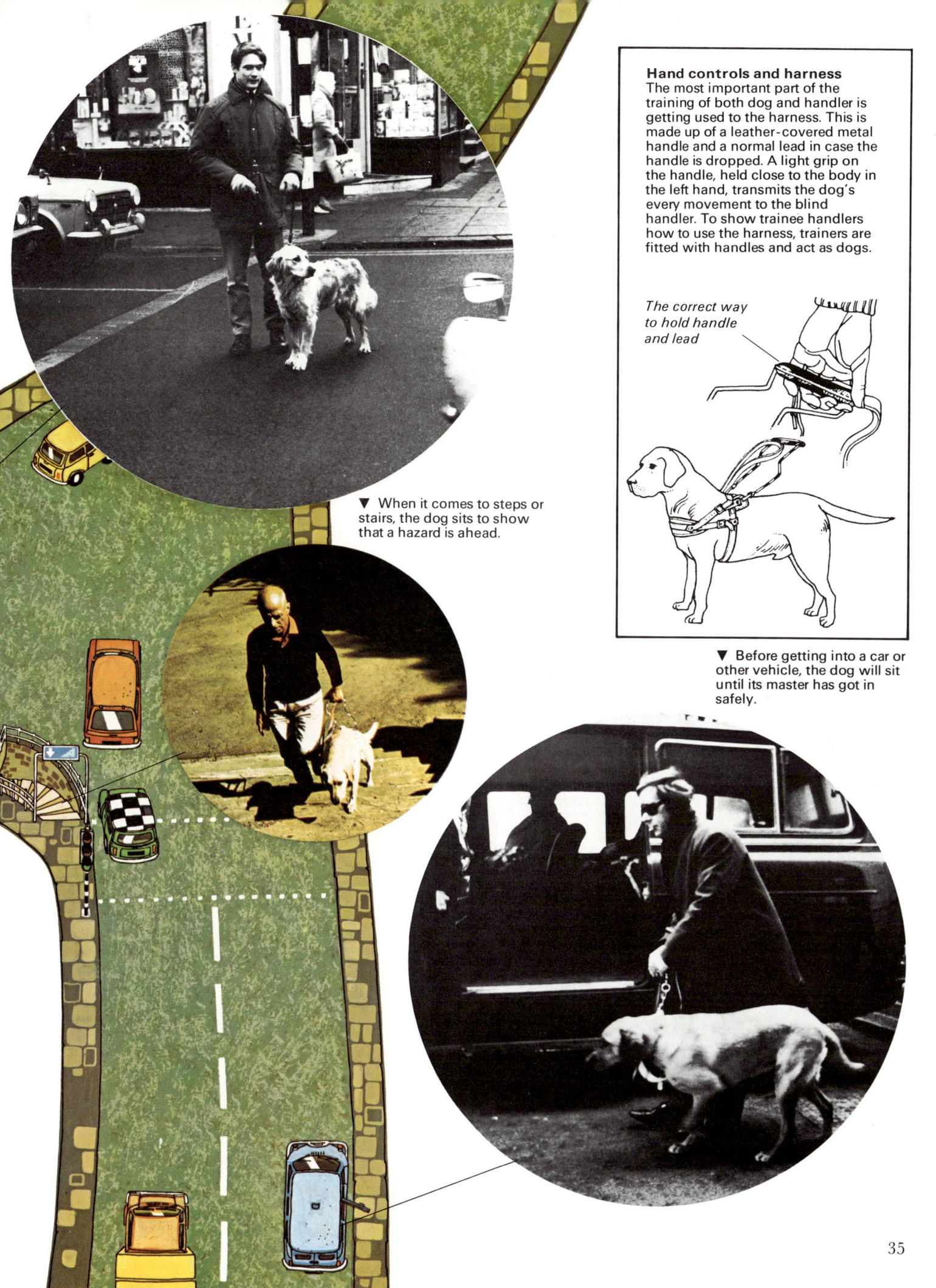

▼ When it comes to steps or stairs, the dog sits to show that a hazard is ahead.

Hand controls and harness
The most important part of the training of both dog and handler is getting used to the harness. This is made up of a leather-covered metal handle and a normal lead in case the handle is dropped. A light grip on the handle, held close to the body in the left hand, transmits the dog's every movement to the blind handler. To show trainee handlers how to use the harness, trainers are fitted with handles and act as dogs.

The correct way to hold handle and lead

▼ Before getting into a car or other vehicle, the dog will sit until its master has got in safely.

Let loose the dogs of war

▲ When the kings of ancient Egypt went to war, large Mastiffs went with them and played a full part in the fighting, as the picture shows.

▼ When gas was used, both dogs and men needed masks. These dogs were among the 28,000 used by the German army in trench warfare in World War I.

▼ This dog has just found a mine. In World War II many dogs were taught to smell out mines and point them out to their handlers.

A fiendish weapon

Terrible tales have been told of the ferocious dogs which went to war with the kings of the ancient world. In Babylonia, these dogs were so important that four cities were let off the payment of taxes provided they bred and trained dogs for the king.

These dogs were used for a variety of purposes. Giant Mastiffs were set on the heels of fleeing armies and the Romans used dogs to send messages from one place to another. A dog would be made to swallow a metal tube containing a message, and when it reached its destination it would be killed and the message removed.

In the Middle Ages, war dogs carried pots of burning resin on their backs and were sent to run under enemy horses. Others had armour fitted with spikes to tear at the horses.

Uses in a modern world

The passing of the Middle Ages seemed to signal the end of war dogs and it seems strange that it was modern, mechanized warfare which brought about their return. The Germans began to use them in the late 19th century, and they were so successful that many other countries took them up.

Today, the job of the war dog is not as bloodthirsty as it was in the past. As guards, cable-layers and Red Cross dogs they are on the fringes of warfare, but are every bit as useful as their ancestors.

▲ After bomb raids in World War II, dogs were taken to destroyed houses to sniff out buried victims. The dog in the small picture was awarded a medal for this work.

▲ Special airborne army units and the medical corps use parachute dogs. It is said that they jump quite happily the first time but are less keen once they know what it is like.

▼ This U.S. airman needs his padded clothing as the dog is trained to attack. Most countries use dogs to guard military bases.

First to the Pole sledge dogs

Sledge dog breeds

▲ The Malamute is the most powerful of the sledge dogs.

▲ Samoyeds are also used to herd sheep.

Husky in a harness

▲ A Husky in its harness. These intelligent dogs are normally chosen to lead the teams.

Northern superdogs

The toughest of all dogs: that is a fair description of the Arctic sledge dogs, which can pull heavy loads over long distances in unbelievably bad conditions. These animals are closer to half-tamed wolves than domestic dogs, but without them many Eskimo tribes could not have survived and Polar exploration would not have been possible until the introduction of modern equipment.

The race for the South Pole

The greatest test of the capabilities of the sledge dog came in 1911, when man first reached the South Pole. Two expeditions set out at the same time, one led by Roald Amundsen, a Norwegian, and the other by Robert Scott, an Englishman.

Amundsen was a firm believer in the sledge dog. He took 52 dogs with him and made sure that his men got to know them and treated them well. But he was also a ruthless man. As the loads of provisions on the sledges dwindled, surplus dogs were shot and their flesh eaten by man and dog alike. Only 11 dogs returned from the expedition.

Scott did not like using the wild Eskimo dogs, and he used other methods to reach the Pole. He arrived in January 1912, but found that Amundsen and his well-trained dogs had beaten him to it. Yet again, the dog had proved its usefulness.

How the teams are harnessed

▶ **Fan trace.** Each dog is harnessed to the sledge with its own trace. This is the old Eskimo way of harnessing but is not used much now.

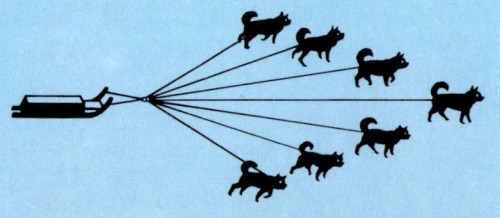

▶ **Centre trace.** A more efficient way of harnessing teams. Pairs of dogs are fastened to a centre trace, with a single leader in front.

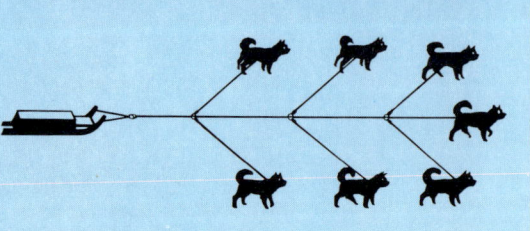

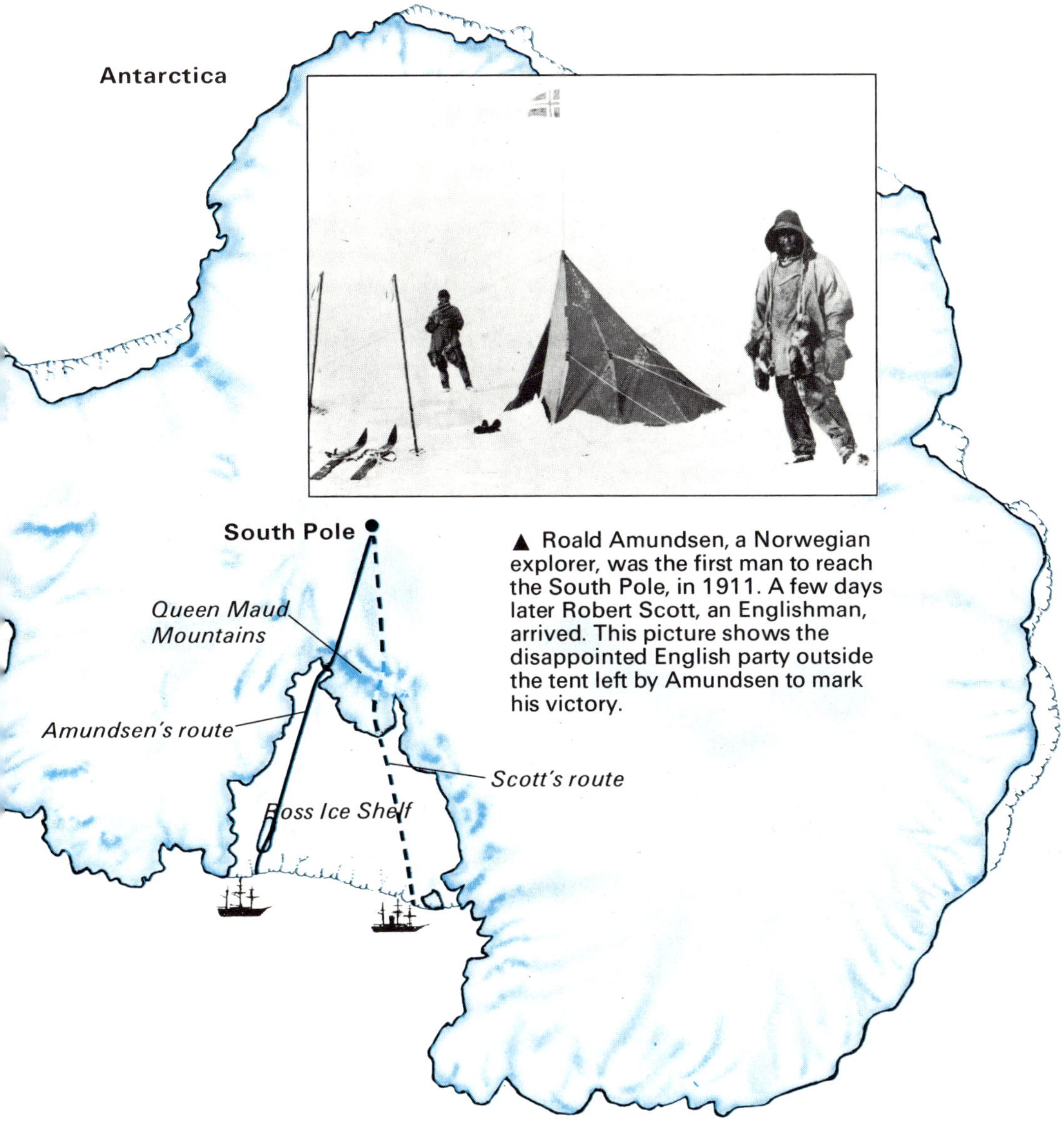

Antarctica
South Pole
Queen Maud Mountains
Amundsen's route
Scott's route
Ross Ice Shelf

▲ Roald Amundsen, a Norwegian explorer, was the first man to reach the South Pole, in 1911. A few days later Robert Scott, an Englishman, arrived. This picture shows the disappointed English party outside the tent left by Amundsen to mark his victory.

Rival explorers

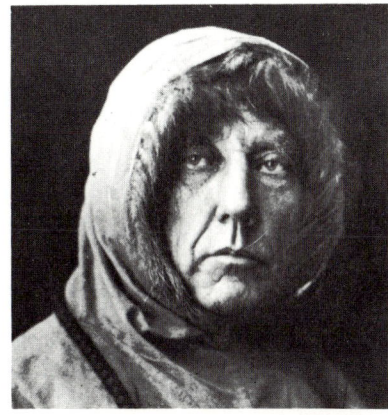

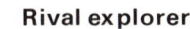

▲ Roald Amundsen (1872–1928). He had great faith in dogs and his team was experienced in handling them. This gave him a big advantage over his English rival.

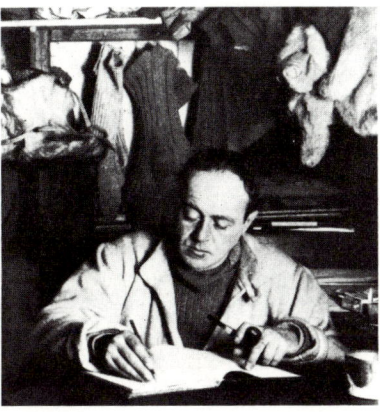

▲ Captain Robert Scott (1868–1912). He and his companions were brave but badly-equipped. They ran into heavy blizzards on their way back and all lost their lives.

▼ Scott distrusted sledge dogs and took ponies to the Antarctic to pull his sledges. When this failed, he and his men had to pull their equipment themselves.

▼ Nowadays, many Polar expeditions use mechanized "sno-cats". Despite this, dogs seem likely to remain important, especially where the ground is rocky.

TRANS ANTARCTIC EXPEDITION

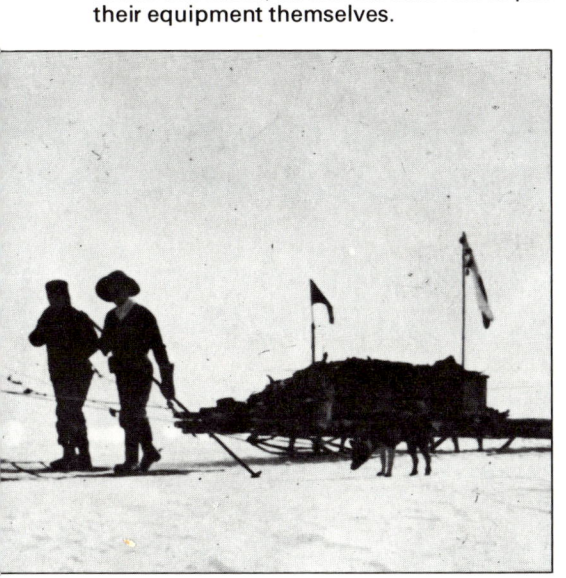

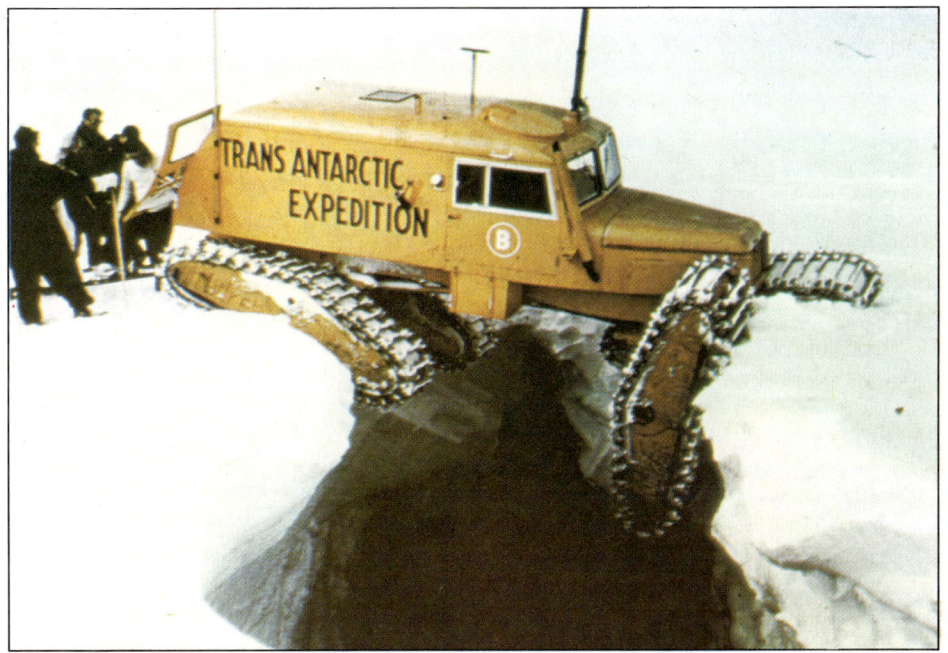

Entertainment with a purpose

A highly skilled job

One of the dog's natural instincts is to herd. But there is a vast difference between the instinct of an untrained dog and the performance of a working sheepdog.

Anyone who has seen a sheepdog trial or display marvels at the skill of these little dogs and at the high level of understanding between them and their handlers. At a sign from his master, a sheepdog can put a flock of perhaps 20 sheep through the most complicated manoeuvres without a sound and without touching a single sheep.

High quality entertainment

The first trials were held in Wales one hundred years ago. They soon became popular and are now held in many parts of the world. Trials are competitions in which shepherds with either one or two dogs have to carry out certain tests in handling sheep.

As well as being good entertainment, sheepdog trials have a serious purpose. Shepherds from all over the world are keen to buy the puppies of animals which have won major events. This raises the standards of sheep dogs and so improves the management of sheep.

1. At a whistle from his master, the dog sets off on a wide run out to collect the first ten sheep. It drives them through the gate and then leaves them while it collects the next ten.

Route of first gather

Penning

4. The dog drives the marked sheep into the pen. This is the most difficult part of the operation as it must also make sure that the rest of the flock does not stray. The shepherd holds the gate of the pen ready to shut it, but neither he nor the dog must touch the sheep.

A sheepdog trial

▲ In Australia, farmers use a local breed called a Kelpie. It has hundreds of sheep to deal with, so the farmer teaches it to climb around on their backs.

▶ Dogs control sheep by staring at them. This is called showing eye and the sheep behave as if hypnotized. But some dogs are too strong-eyed and will lie staring at the sheep instead of moving them.

2. The dog collects the second ten sheep and drives them through the gate to join the first ten. The dog must move them steadily and without panic.

Route of second gather

Triangular drive

Shedding

3. Next comes the triangular drive. The sheep are driven behind the shepherd, through the two gates and back to the middle. Then the dog separates some marked sheep from the flock. This is called shedding.

Five marked sheep

8,000 years of Salukis

► Many ancient Egyptian paintings show Salukis as the hunting dogs of kings. This one dates from 1350 BC. The Saluki was by then already an ancient and highly-valued breed.

▼ A Persian miniature showing a pet Saluki with a jewelled collar. All over the East, Salukis were kept as pets by royal families, and they were the only dogs the Arabs would allow inside their homes.

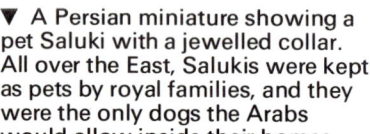

A typical member of the dog family

The beautiful Saluki is believed by many people to be the oldest breed of dog. To tell its story is to tell the story of the domestic dog itself, for the history of the Saluki sums up all that the dog has gained or lost from its life with man.

Dogs were first used by man for hunting. The oldest known painting of a dog with a huntsman is 8,000 years old and shows a Saluki-like hound. This was found in the deserts of the Middle East, where the breed developed.

Man soon discovered that the dog was adaptable, that is that it could be altered to suit different conditions. Salukis were ideal dogs in desert conditions and the Arabs who bred them were careful to preserve their good qualities. The Saluki has also been crossed with other breeds to produce new dogs for man's pleasure.

A survivor from the past

Over the years, the tasks which the dog can perform for man have been taken over by machines, and their lives have changed considerably. Although some still work, most dogs are now kept as pets. The open country from which they came is vanishing, and they are unable to get the exercise they need in towns and cities.

In the past, the dog has proved to be a successful and adaptable animal, but it has now given up its independence and relies on man. Dogs are a relic of man's distant past. What will be their place in his future?

▲ Like many modern dogs, the Saluki has largely outlived its use. Few now hunt. Most are kept only for their beauty and companionship.

▼ This Saluki, at work with a Jordanian Frontier Patrol in 1960, is in its element in the arid desert surroundings.

▲ The ears of the Saluki are naturally long and feathered, but they are sometimes cropped. This was introduced for dogs which hunted jackals in the desert. Long ears provided an easy hold for the jackal, so they were cropped short.

▲ The Borzoi is a breed created by man 300 years ago. Salukis were taken to Russia to hunt wolves, but died in the cold winter. A Saluki was then crossed with a Russian Collie and the result was the Borzoi, a dog with the speed of the Saluki and the thick coat of the Collie.

43

Projects find out more about dogs

Keeping a scrapbook

You can easily produce an interesting book of your own about dogs. There is a great deal to be found out about dogs even though they have lived with man for so long. Because we are so used to them, we often do not really notice what they do. Your study could turn up something new and might earn thanks from scientists in the future.

Start by studying the dogs of your own area. You may be surprised to find how commercially important they are. Check the advertisements about dogs in your local newspaper. Are there any kennels locally? Do these breed dogs or merely board them? Are there any pet shops in the area? Which dogs command the best prices? How much dog food is sold? How many shops sell it? Other questions to answer might be the number of entrants in local dog shows, attendance at dog training classes, the use made of dogs by the local police and their breeds, what happens to strays and how many of these there are each year.

After this, take a dog census of your home area to find out the most popular breeds. Choose a site to work from and equip yourself with a book to help you identify the breeds, some pencils and squared paper. Draw a column on the paper in which to write the names of each breed of dog. For each breed that you can identify shade in a square for each specimen of the breed that you see.

You can produce other graphs to show the results of breed popularity tests. Ask a given number of people to name the dog each likes best.

Follow this up by making your own observations of these favourites. Watch as long as you can. How do different breeds react to the same stimulus? You can use anything from a rattled tin to a sudden whistle but do not tease the dogs or frighten them. Concentrate on one of these dogs, or your own if you have one, and make a study of its many different barks and tail wags and the sort of situation that causes each of them. When is the tail wagged fast and when slowly? When is it wagged high or low or to one side? Follow and record a complete sequence of events, such as the meeting of two dogs. Does this always follow the same pattern? Map the territory marked out by a dog and note its reactions to other dogs within the area.

It is important to keep accurate notes of all that you see and do. If possible, illustrate these notes with sketches and photographs.

How well does it smell?

This is a simple experiment to test your dog's sense of smell. Train the dog to fetch a thrown stick. Always use the same stick, marked in some way so that it can be identified. Next, throw this stick into a pile of others of the same size and shape. Does the dog bring back the right one?

Now place the marked stick on the pile and ask someone else to throw another one on. Does your dog fetch the thrown stick or the marked one?

Another variation of this test is for the marked stick to be thrown on the pile by someone other than yourself. If you have a friend with a dog of a different breed you can compare their performances.

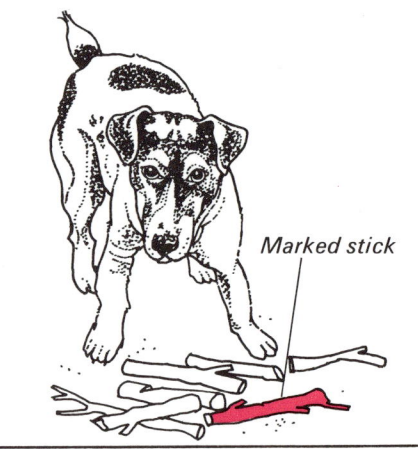

Marked stick

Testing a dog's memory

Put out several upturned tins or other containers. Let your dog see you put a piece of some favourite food under one of these. Now release the dog. It will probably go straight to the container hiding the food.

Repeat the experiment a little later on and increase the time between hiding the food and releasing the dog to search for it. Continue the process and keep an accurate record of the experiments to see how long it can remember the right container.

So far the dog has relied on its sense of smell to find the food. To make sure that it relies on memory and not on its sense of smell, put the food under each of the containers in turn for a time. In this way all three containers will smell of food. Then try the experiment again.

WARNING
When dealing with dogs, remember that not all of them are friendly and many that want to be friendly may also be nervous. Never force your friendship on a dog.

Do not hold out your hand with the fingers outstretched. If the dog shows an interest in you, let it first sniff at the back of your hand. Do not touch it until it seems really at ease with you and avoid the scruff of its neck. Stroke the shoulder and gradually move your hand to its head.

First Aid

Every dog owner should know something about first aid and what to do in case of emergency. Prompt treatment can often prevent simple injuries developing into something serious.

But remember that these are only emergency measures. All except the very simplest of injuries should be shown to a vet as soon as possible. The aim of first aid is to help the vet, not to replace him.

How to make a muzzle

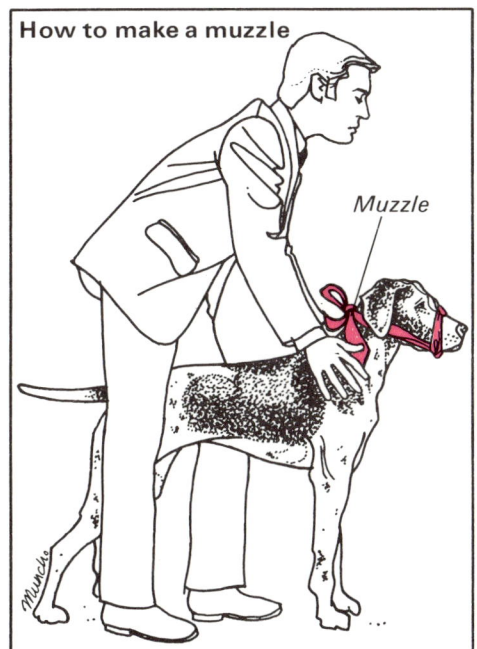

To prevent an injured dog biting, a make-shift muzzle can be made with a tie or bandage formed into a double loop. Pass the loop over the jaws with the ends hanging down, pull these up behind the ears and tie firmly. Remember this is for short term use only.

Giving medicines

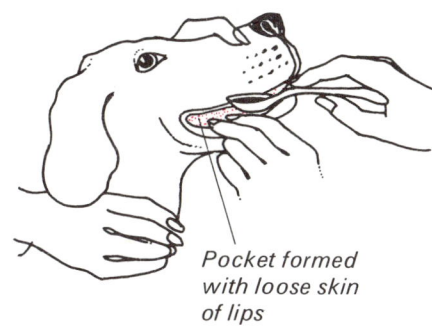

Pocket formed with loose skin of lips

To give pills to a dog you must make it open its mouth. To do this, place your hand over his upper jaw and gently press the lips inwards where the jaws meet. When the dog opens its mouth, tip it slightly backwards. Put the pill as far back on the tongue as you can. Close the mouth and hold it shut, keeping the head up. Stroke the dog's throat and he will swallow the pill.

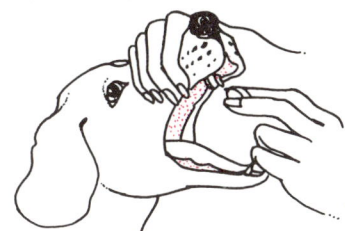

Giving pills

If a dog needs liquid medicine, do not give it to him mixed up with his food as he will probably not eat it. Giving a dog medicine looks very complicated, but with a bit of practice it should become easier.

Hold the dog's mouth closed and his head up. A dog's lips are usually loose at the sides. Gently pull out this loose skin to form a pocket. Pour the medicine slowly into his pouch and allow it to run to the back of the throat. Only pour small amounts at a time, allowing the dog to swallow each dose. To encourage it to swallow, gently rub its throat.

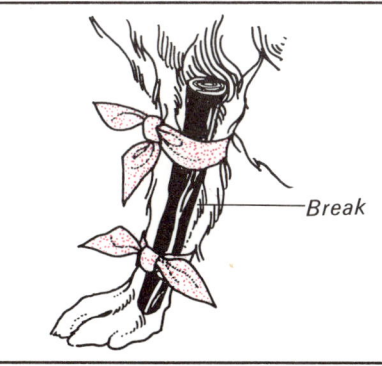

Break

Splints

A ruler or a stick of the right length makes a good emergency splint. The leg must be in a natural position with the splint put along it as comfortably as possible. It should be tied firmly but gently in place, first as near the top of the leg as possible and then at the bottom. Handkerchiefs can be used for this purpose. If possible, cover both legs and splint with a bandage.

Making a stretcher

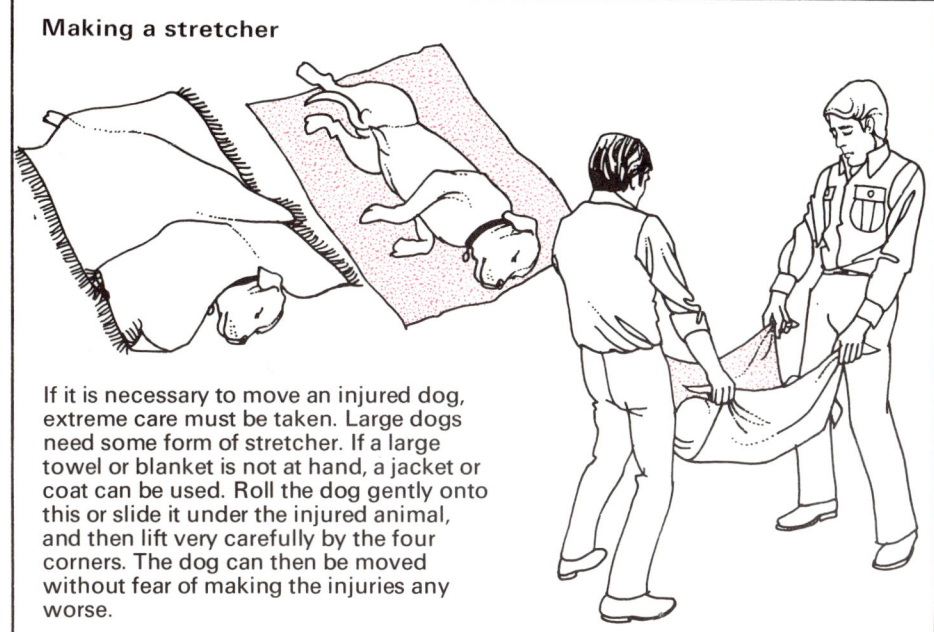

If it is necessary to move an injured dog, extreme care must be taken. Large dogs need some form of stretcher. If a large towel or blanket is not at hand, a jacket or coat can be used. Roll the dog gently onto this or slide it under the injured animal, and then lift very carefully by the four corners. The dog can then be moved without fear of making the injuries any worse.

Objects caught in the throat

If a dog is worrying at its mouth and producing a lot of saliva, it may have a bone or piece of wood wedged across its mouth, between its teeth. This is quite a common injury and can be very serious. The dog probably cannot eat. Luckily, such an object can usually be removed with the handle end of a spoon or with a finger. The dog's mouth must be kept open until this object is well outside or it will very likely swallow it. If a needle or anything sharp becomes stuck in its mouth, a dog must be taken to the vet for treatment.

Injection records

The dog can be protected by injections against a number of diseases. The most important of these is probably distemper. Puppies are usually vaccinated at about twelve weeks and get booster shots one year later. It is a good idea to keep a careful record of exactly what shots have been given and when.

Reference how to describe a dog

Muzzles

Show judges study muzzles carefully. Some breeds are expected to have deep square muzzles and others long, sharp ones. Each type of muzzle has a correct name. Undershot means that the lower jaw is longer than the upper, so that the lower incisors overlap the upper teeth. Overshot is the opposite. Some dogs, such as the Bulldog, should be undershot, but in others it is a fault.

A dog with a curved muzzle rising to a high nose tip is said to be dishfaced. One with a downward sloping nose is downfaced. Pointers are slightly dishfaced and Bull Terriers are clearly downfaced.

These shapes must not be exaggerated. A muzzle that is too long and narrow is said to be snipy and is a bad fault.

Muzzles

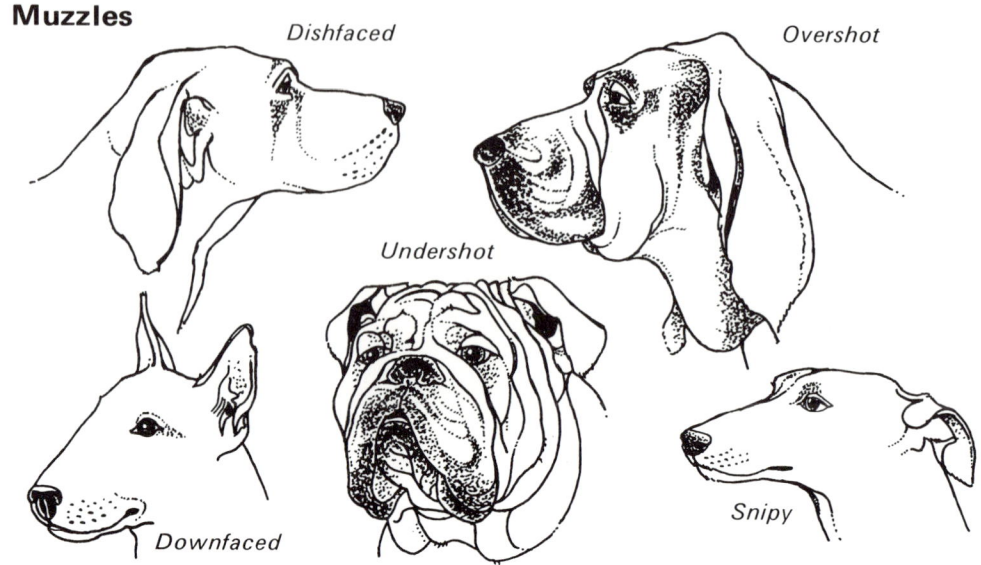

Ears

Each of the different ear shapes has its own name. Bat ears stand up from the head and face forwards. Prick ears also stand up but are more pointed. If the top part of the ear bends forward, it is semi-prick. Erect ears can be more open and tulip shaped.

An ear that hangs down flat and close to the cheek is a drop ear. A button ear is one that has the top part folded over. Small thin ears which fold inwards at the back are known as rose ears.

In some countries, certain dogs have their ears cut to the shape considered right for their breeds. These are then known as crop ears. In other countries this is banned.

Ears

Tails

When a dog has its tail cut short it is said to be docked. If it is docked very short it is left with a bobtail. In some breeds the tail curls tightly over the back. This is a ringtail.

A tail carried high up over the back is said to be gay. The reverse is a down tail, which is long and hangs between the legs. If it is very thick at the base with thick, short hair, it is an otter tail. A rat tail is also thick at the root but the tip has little or no hair. The plumed tail of the setter is called a flag.

A very bushy tail is a brush. One carried straight and stiffly pointed is a whip tail. A screw tail is one that is short and badly shaped and a crooked one is said to be crank.

Tails

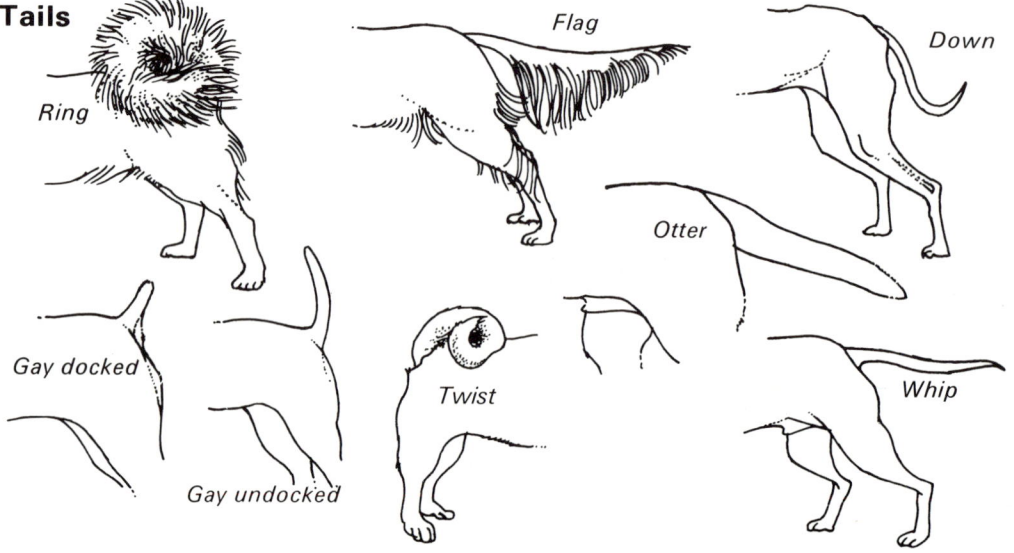

Index

Illustration Credits

Key to the positions of illustrations: (T) top, (C) centre, (B) bottom, and combinations: for example (TR) top right, or (CL) centre left.

Artists
Peter Connolly: 4-5, 23 (B), 40-1
Eric Jewell Ass.: 8-9, 24, 38 (B), 39
Malcolm McGregor: 18-9
Janet Munch/Freelance Presentations: 34-5, 44-5, 46
Tony Payne: 6-7
Melvyn Raymond: 14-5, 21, 38 (T), 42
John Shackell: 20-1, 22, 23 (T), 28
John Smith: 3, 17, 30-1
Maurice Wilson: 10-1, 12

Photographs and Prints
A.F.A. Colour Library: 8 (L)
A.G.I.P.: 16 (B)
Algerian Tourist Office: 3 (T)
Anglia Survival: 9 (L), 12 (R)
Australian News & Information Bureau: 41 (L & R)
Barnaby's Picture Library: 22
Bibliotheque Nationale: 24 (T)
Bodleian Library: 42 (B)
G. D. Brauns: 16 (T)
Camera Press: 27 (TL)
Central Press Photos Ltd.: 27 (TR), 37 (T)
Commissioner of Police of the Metropolis: 20 (L), 33 (T & C)
Anne Cumbers: 7 (BC), 33 (BR)

Danot: 28 (R)
Foto Lindberg: 39 (TR)
John Freeman: 18
Su Gooders/Ardea Photographics: 13 (TR), 17 (BR)
Greyhound Association: 27 (CL)
Guide dogs for the Blind: 34, 35 (C)
Historic Dog Features: 13 (TL, CR & BR)
Imperial War Museum: 36 (BR), 37 (BL)
John Slater Photography: 27 (BL)
F. L. Kennet/George Rainbird Ltd.: 36 (T)
M. Lowring: 7 (BL & BR)
Mansell Collection: 3 (BR), 31 (T), 39 (TL), 39 (CR)
Mary Evans Picture Library: 17 (TL), 25 (T), 31 (B)
Metropolitan Museum of Art, New York: 42 (T)
National Film Archive: 26 (BL)
National Newspaper Syndicate, Chicago: 28 (L)
Novosti Press Agency: 24 (BR)
Peter Way Ltd.: 12 (L), 35 (T & B)
Picturepoint: 9 (R)
Pictorial Press: 26 (T), 32 (L), 33 (BL), 37 (BR)
Radio Times Hulton Picture Library: 20 (R), 24 (BL), 32 (R), 38-9 (C)
Roger-Viollet: 19, 21, 36 (BL)
Syndication International: 16 (C), 26 (BR), 27 (BR), 43 (B)
The Times: 43 (T)
Tierbilder Okapia: 8 (R)
Trans-Antarctic Association: 39 (BR)
United Features Syndicate Inc.: 28 (B)
University of Toronto: 25 (B)
Walt Disney Productions: 29
Michael Wright: 17 (BL)

proost Turnhout (Belgium)